How To Start A Successful Law Practice

The New Lawyer's Guide To Opening An Office As A Solo Or Small Firm Attorney

William L. Pfeifer, Jr.

First Edition

Pipers Willow, Inc.
Sheridan, Wyoming

D1157140

How To Start A Successful Law Practice
The New Lawyer's Guide To Opening An Office
As A Solo Or Small Firm Attorney
by William L. Pfeifer, Jr.

Copyright © 2006 by William L. Pfeifer, Jr.

Published by:
Pipers Willow, Inc.
Sheridan, Wyoming

ISBN: 0-9787277-0-3

Library of Congress Control Number: 2006933570

Typeset by Jaspal Singh Bisht at Aruna Enterprises, Delhi, India

Printed in the United States of America.

All rights reserved. Printed in the United States of America. No part of this book may be reproduced or transmitted in any form or by any means, electronic or mechanical, including photocopying, recording or by any information storage and retrieval system, without written permission from the author, except for the inclusions of brief quotations in a review.

The author and publisher specifically disclaim any responsibility for any liability, loss, or risk, personal or otherwise, which is incurred as a consequence, directly or indirectly, of the use and application of any of the contents of this book. This book contains only ideas and opinions, and is sold with the understanding that the author and publisher are not engaged in rendering professional services in the book. If the reader requires personal assistance or advice, a competent professional should be consulted. Although every precaution has been taken in the preparation of this book, there may be mistakes or there may be information which has become outdated by the time the reader reviews the contents. The publisher and author assume no responsibility for errors or omissions.

For information, write to Pipers Willow, Inc., 1617 N. Main St., Suite B, Sheridan, WY 82801.

DEDICATION

To Yuan Liu, for filling my life with joy, inspiration, and love.

TABLE OF CONTENTS

INTRODUCTION

This book is written for the new lawyer who does not want to go to work for a firm, and for the experienced lawyer who dreams of making a new start on his or her own. After four years of college and three years of law school, and often even after working as a law clerk or as an associate in a firm, most new lawyers are clueless about how to start their own law practice. Law school teaches students how to find the answers to legal questions, but it fails to provide much instruction on how to go out and hang up a shingle. This book shows how to start and succeed with your own firm, and shows you how to get started without spending a fortune.

Starting a law practice can be challenging, stressful, and financially difficult at times. Contrary to popular opinion, it is not an easy "road to riches." Lawyers have to work hard and earn their success, and new lawyers should understand that it may be several years before they reap the rewards of their investment. But most lawyers who have started a solo practice or formed their own small firm will say that the results were well worth the sacrifice and effort. Nothing is better than being your own boss, setting your own hours, selecting a specialty, and deciding for yourself which cases you will take and which ones you will reject. It is the lawyer's version of being an entrepreneur, and it is a great way to practice law.

Undertaking this kind of venture is not a short-term commitment. Building a successful law practice takes time and patience. It also takes proper planning. This book will not teach you how to be patient during the slow times (and there will be slow times), but it can teach you how to plan for both short-term and long-term success.

The lessons in this book come from the real-world experience of solo and small firm attorneys. Some of the ideas come from my own personal experience, and other recommendations have been gleaned from the advice and experiences of others. Each person is different, every attorney has had unique experiences, no two personalities are exactly alike, and what works for some may not work for others. Use your best judgment in deciding which parts of this book will work best for you and which strategies you will apply towards your success.

The traditional approach of a book like this would be to waste time and paper making the first chapter of this book about whether you should start your own law practice. We could consider characteristics of a person who starts his or her own law firm; the pros and cons of starting a practice; the financial risks and the financial rewards; and all of the other factors people consider when deciding whether to open an office. My belief is that no book can tell you whether to make a decision like this, and you do not need a chapter of pep talk for you to get started. Certain risks and benefits are addressed in the context of other topics, but this book presupposes that you have decided to start your own law practice, and goes straight into showing you how to do it.

Here's what you'll find in *How to Build a Successful Law Practice:*

Chapter One, **Choosing An Area Of Practice**, asks "what kind of lawyer are you," and helps you find the answer.

Chapter Two, **Legal Specialties**, provides an overview of the major specialty and sub-specialty areas of law.

Chapter Three, **Selecting An Office Location**, addresses the factors to consider in choosing the place to operate your business.

Chapter Four, **Choosing A Form Of Business**, explores the basic forms of business entities used by attorneys to operate their practices.

Chapter Five, **Setting Up A Business**, takes you through the essential steps involved in formally creating your business.

Chapter Six, **Office Furniture, Equipment, And Supplies**, reviews what you need to equip and operate your new law firm.

Chapter Seven, **Selecting Stationary**, addresses the importance of professionalism in your written communications.

Chapter Eight, **Setting And Collecting Fees**, explains how to establish your fees and then collect them from your clients.

Chapter Nine, **Hiring A Secretary**, reviews the factors to consider in deciding when you are ready to hire a secretary, and what qualities to look for when you do.

Chapter Ten, **Marketing Your Practice**, teaches you how to bring in clients by making yourself known in the community.

Chapter Eleven, **Legal Research**, shows where you can find the free and paid resources you need for legal research.

And Chapter Twelve - **Sample Forms**, provides some basic law practice forms to help you get your office up and running with professionalism and efficiency.

As mentioned before, all attorneys are different, and what is a match for one may not be a match for another. With that in mind, some sections of this book present options and the pros and cons of each, rather than spelling out only one way of doing things. There are many paths to success, and the new lawyer must choose which way works the best for him or her. It is my hope that these sections of the book will not only show you how to get started with building your law practice, but that they will also stimulate your own creative thinking process.

If you are serious about transforming your life and fulfilling the dream of having your own law practice, then turn the page and get started.

CHAPTER ONE

Choosing an Area of Practice

"What kind of lawyer are you?"

In order to turn introductions into new clients, you must be able to answer this question with confidence. Yet an amazing number of attorneys get the "deer in the headlights" look when asked to describe what they do. Whether out of actual interest or merely to make polite conversation, most people will ask what kind of law you practice, and they will assume you can answer this question relatively easily. You never hear doctors stammering around trying to describe their specialty field of medicine, but many attorneys, even with years of experience under their belt, get tongue-tied when asked to describe the work they do every day. This can result from the attorney being afraid of losing a potential client by not naming the area of law that matches the person's needs, or it could be the result of the attorney having no clear picture of his or her professional identity. Often it is a combination of both.

Many attorneys attempt to dodge the question by responding, "what kind of lawyer do you need?" This humorous answer may lead the potential client to describe a legal issue on his mind. You may hear, "Well, I have been thinking about updating my will," or "I need to consult with an attorney about a divorce." In those situations, the deflection of the question may work, and can lead to being hired by a new client. But many other times the person does

5

not have an immediate need for a lawyer, and the question is simply out of curiosity. Your job in that situation is to make a positive impression so that when that person does need an attorney, he or she thinks of you.

In order to make yourself more memorable, the better approach is to describe your practice in specialized terms beyond the labels of "lawyer" or "attorney." "I'm a criminal defense lawyer," or "I'm a tax attorney," will be more impressive and stand out in someone's memory far longer than "I do a little bit of everything." If you are trying to appear to be a specialist, but still want to keep your options open with that person, you could say something like, "I primarily handle family law issues, but I also represent people with issues involving real estate, criminal defense, personal injury, and civil matters." That is close to saying "I have a general practice," but it sounds more specific and gives your prospective client a better image of what you do.

If you already have experience in a particular area of law from working in a firm, or perhaps from a different career prior to law school, then it may be easy to choose an area of specialization. Such a background may also be a good source of referrals for your new practice. Connections in the corporate world can be particularly useful in landing clients with ongoing legal needs, providing a much-needed steady flow of income. Most individuals only need the services of an attorney once or twice in their lives, but businesses need attorneys quite frequently. A background in the business world can open doors in that community and can provide an advantage in bringing stability to your income early in your practice.

Most attorneys beginning their practice do not have a specialized background that would create an instant niche market for their services. The majority of lawyers start their new practice with a great deal of uncertainty as to who will be their clientele and what they will do for them. Many new attorneys are glad to have any clients come into the office regardless of the service needed, and are more concerned with paying the bills than with developing a particular specialty. When the phone bill is due and the landlord is asking for the rent, you may find yourself handling cases outside of any area that ever crossed your mind in law school.

Some new lawyers will attempt to select an area of specialization from the start, only to find that the market for those services is too small or that he or she does not actually like handling that kind of work. Other lawyers take the position that they have a general practice, and will represent anyone who walks in the door. Those lawyers often find it difficult to answer the "what kind of lawyer are you" question, and may have trouble attracting clients with anything more than the most routine legal questions. Nonetheless, starting as a general practitioner is often the best way for the new lawyer to begin a practice. This is particularly true if you do not have a marketable niche background or do not have a clear vision of what kind of cases you want to handle. The beginning of your practice is the best time to determine which areas of law you like and which areas you dislike, and it is also the best time to start understanding the local legal market. When first starting a practice, the new lawyer is not likely to be in a position to turn away much paying business anyway, so take the opportunity to experiment and discover areas of talent and interest.

When first leaving law school, the young lawyer's opinion as to what kind of lawyer he or she will be may be drastically different than the lawyer with a few years of experience. For example, many lawyers learn that they cannot stand handling divorce and child custody cases. Such cases can be emotionally draining, the clients can be intolerable, and the stakes are often very high. On the other hand, some attorneys find that the opportunity to help and influence the lives of others in such a direct and personal way is very rewarding, and they thrive on helping people cope with their personal struggles. Many attorneys believe they could never be involved in criminal defense, and then discover how gratifying it can be to help someone get a fresh start on life. Some lawyers may decide that they cannot sit in an office drafting legal documents, and yearn for the excitement of the courtroom; others may desire the stability and flexibility of a paper practice where they do not have to run back and forth to the courthouse. These are not things that the new lawyer can learn while daydreaming in a law school class; they are only learned by actually "taking a test drive" in different areas of law.

A good approach for a new attorney is to start building a practice around a few key areas of interest. If possible, limit yourself to no more than three or four fields of law that interest you. This will allow enough diversity in your practice to maintain sufficient cash flow in the early days of your practice, but will also provide an escape from the impossible task of being an expert on everything. Over time, this may condense down to one or two areas of practice, but the new lawyer should allow for some flexibility while crafting a professional identity. Unless you came into the profession with some niche background that provides a strong built-in client basis, you need to keep some of your options open in the early years of your practice.

There are some who recommend being as specialized as possible from day one, even going beyond picking one field of practice to having only very specified areas of expertise within that one field. The rationale is that while this will reduce the overall number of people who are considering your services, it will make you stand out among other attorneys to those who need an expert in the specific area of law you handle. For example, an attorney who establishes himself as the local condominium law expert may not get many calls from other kinds of clients, but before long he could have a corner on the condo market.

While there is some wisdom in this approach, it can be risky to become too specialized too early, especially if the attorney is attempting to carve out too narrow a niche. For example, if an attorney took out a yellow pages advertisement stating that he or she specialized in grandparent visitation rights, that attorney's practice could be in trouble if the state's grandparent visitation statute was struck down as unconstitutional. Changes in the workers compensation statutes in some states have made that area of law become less profitable over time, to the point that some attorneys have stopped handling those cases at all. It only takes one court ruling or one act of the legislature to dramatically affect your law practice, so always keep that in mind when defining the scope of your selected specialty. Additionally, it could be a major mistake to specialize too early in your practice, only to find that there is not much of a market for that particular niche in your community. It serves no practical benefit to be the recognized expert in the community if members of the community do not need that kind of legal service.

Some attorneys do very well by advertising that their "practice is limited to matters of criminal defense," or that they are a "certified family law specialist."[1] This certainly makes sense, when one draws a comparison to the medical profession. Given a choice between a general practice physician and a cardiologist, most people would choose the cardiologist to perform their heart surgery. Likewise, few people would hire a cardiologist to treat them for cancer, but would select the oncologist who specializes in treating that illness.

---

[1] Rules regarding the use of terms such as "specialist" vary from state to state, and some state bar associations prohibit attorneys from claiming that they "specialize" in anything. Review your state's rules of professional conduct to determine what phrasing is acceptable in your jurisdiction.

Another important issue to consider is the size of your marketplace. If you are in a large city, it is much easier to specialize than when you are in a small community. If you are a "small town lawyer," your clients will expect you to handle all of their legal needs. Thus, you may write a client's will one year, handle his car wreck case the next year, a divorce a few years after that, and perhaps even probate his estate after his death. If the client owns a small business, you may find yourself handling their collections, forming an S-corporation, or drafting business contracts. A small community is a great place to open a practice, but be prepared to keep your practice more general than you would in a big city environment.

If you have chosen to start out with a general practice, make it your goal to begin narrowing your practice after the first year or two, so that you can sculpt your practice to match the life you really want. By that time, you will have represented enough clients to have an idea of what interests you and of where your talents lie. If you find a case to be particularly interesting, consider whether it is just the specific case, or whether you have actually found an area of law that excites you. The more narrowly you can define your practice, the easier it will be to target the clientele you wish to serve, but do not narrow your options too much until you know what you really want to do.

While the next chapter lists and defines the primary legal specialties, it is difficult to name every legal specialty that exists because so many specialties overlap or exist within well-defined niche markets. A good approach in trying to select a specialty is, when possible, to draw upon past education and experience to find a focus for your practice. The practicality of this may be determined by the geographical setting in which your practice is located, as well as other circumstances related to the area of specialty (such as a need for further academic training). Also, your long-term success will be heavily affected by your degree of job satisfaction. Consequently, it is important to spend some time figuring out what your "dream practice" would look like, and determining a path to get as close to that practice as possible. Set measurable goals, and monitor your progress on developing not only the practice, but on having the life you really want. You have gone out on your own so that you can control your career and your life, so make sure to actually make your life what you want it to be.

CHAPTER TWO

Legal Specialties

In order to select an area or areas of legal specialization, it is helpful to have an idea of some of the choices available to you. The following is a description of the major legal specialties you could consider in building your practice. It is hard for one area of law to function without touching on other areas, so many of the described areas overlap with each other, and often contain crossing sub-specialties as well. Remember that any specific issue within a specialty or sub-specialty can be developed into a niche practice, given the right circumstances.

Administrative Law

Administrative law deals with the administrative and regulatory authority of governmental agencies over a wide variety of matters. Attorneys working in this area must be familiar with the rules, regulations, and procedures of governmental agencies, such as the Social Security Administration and the Department of Labor. They will be involved in presenting claims to these agencies, or in defending organizations from claims filed against them.

Admiralty and Maritime Law

If it happens on the water, it probably falls under admiralty law. This legal specialty addresses issues related to navigation and shipping, which can include a broad range of matters such as insurance, personal injury, liens, towing, and recreation.

Antitrust and Unfair Competition

Antitrust laws regulate competition in the marketplace. Monopolies, unfair trade practices, predatory practices, mergers, and advertising are all issues that arise in this area of law.

Appellate Practice

At the end of a trial, someone loses, and that person or entity has the right to appeal that loss to a higher court. While there are certain limited issues which receive a *de novo*[2] review by appellate courts, most appeals revolve around whether the trial court made an error of law or misapplied the law to the facts. In appellate work there is no discovery process, oral argument is rare in most appellate courts, all issues are decided based upon the record of the proceedings before the lower court, and the case is almost always argued solely through written briefs. Appellate briefs must adhere to specific rules and formats, and the rules governing form and structure must be strictly followed.

---

[2] For those who slipped through law school without learning their Latin terminology, *de novo* means anew, and refers to reviewing an issue as if it has not been heard before and as if no decision had ever been rendered.

Aviation Law

The federal and state governments have enacted laws governing aircraft and aviation facilities, and there are government agencies designated to regulate air traffic. Most aviation law falls under federal authority, and will be overseen by appropriate federal agencies.

Banking

Banks and bank accounts are regulated by both state and federal law. Negotiable instruments, certificates of deposit, FDIC issues, lending issues, secured and commercial transactions, and any other matters typically handled by banks will fall under this general area of practice. Numerous sub-specializations exist in this area as well.

Bankruptcy

The practice of bankruptcy law involves assisting debtors who have become insolvent, or assisting the creditors of those debtors who are seeking to minimize their financial loss. When the debts of a person or a business exceed their ability to pay their creditors, then the debtor may file a voluntary petition for bankruptcy, or the creditors may file an involuntary petition to force bankruptcy upon the debtor. In a consumer bankruptcy, the debtor's assets may be liquidated to pay off the creditors in a "Chapter 7" proceeding, or the debts may be restructured into a manageable payment plan at a reduced percentage of the debt load under "Chapter 13." In a commercial bankruptcy, debtors must utilize the complex process of "Chapter 11," which is considered by many to be a specialty in itself.

Business Law

Also commonly known as "corporate law" or "commercial law," business law incorporates a broad range of matters related to the operation of various forms of business. A business may be formal or informal, a corporation or a sole proprietorship, a partnership or a limited liability company, or some other entity. If the activity or entity is designed to make a profit, then it will fall under business law. This is necessarily a broad category of law practice, and can involve matters related to banking, bankruptcy, credit, contracts, employment, real estate, sales, secured transactions, and any other area related to carrying on business activities.

Civil Litigation

Civil litigation is the practice of being a "trial lawyer." Civil litigation generally refers to the practice of filing or defending lawsuits related to civil wrongs. Litigation of disputes can be related to any area of law, including criminal law where the criminal allegations serve as the basis or a factor in a civil suit (such as a personal injury suit against a drunk driver who caused injuries to others). Civil litigation requires the ability to think on one's feet, extensive knowledge of the rules of evidence, and the ability to remain calm in the courtroom. Litigation is an adversarial proceeding, involves conflict and confronta-

16

tion, and can be stressful to all persons involved, but it can also be quite exciting to those who enjoy the challenge.

Communications

Communications law revolves around the laws governing radio and television broadcasting. Practice in this area will involve substantial dealings with the Federal Communications Commission (FCC), which grants licenses, enacts rules, and provides oversight for radio, television, wire, satellite, and cable.

Constitutional Law/ Civil Rights

Constitutional law, also known as civil rights law, involves protecting and interpreting those rights guaranteed to persons by the United States Constitution. These rights have also been expanded upon through certain acts of legislation as well as by court interpretation. Litigation in this area involves a vast array of issues, each of which can be developed into a legal specialty of its own. Issues such as freedom of speech, freedom of religion, abortion rights and restrictions, affirmative action, sexual harassment, discrimination, exercising the right to vote, same sex marriages, the Patriot Act, equal access to public schools and facilities, and fair treatment of individuals by law enforcement authorities and the courts are among the topics which fall within constitutional and civil rights law.

Construction

In general, construction law deals with matters related to the improvement, development, and maintenance of real estate. Construction law crosses several areas of the law, such as real estate, contracts, torts, business, taxation, labor law, and secured transactions. An attorney handling construction law issues will commonly deal with disputes between contractors and subcontractors, the filing and release of liens, insurance coverage, and the drafting and interpretation of contracts.

Contracts

Contract law deals with the creation of contracts and then dealing with their legal implications and consequences. Contracts are agreements between people or organizations to do or refrain from doing certain actions. While most contracts are written documents (no matter how informally), they can also be based on oral agreements as long as they are not in violation of the applicable version of the Statute of Frauds. Attorneys in contract law will address issues such as the adequacy and/or lack of consideration, the competency of the parties to the contract, whether fraud or duress was involved, the interpretation and enforceability of the terms of the contract, what constitutes breach of the contract, and the right to terminate the agreement.

Computer Law

One of the newer areas of law practice, computer law deals with issues involved with electronic data and computer usage.

This area may involve computer sales or usage in commerce, or it may involve issues such as computer crimes or misuse, theft of trade secrets or intellectual property, internet pornography, data encryption or destruction, electronic discovery, and any other ways in which computers are involved in transactions or events.

Criminal Law

Attorneys can work in criminal law as prosecutors, as defense attorneys, and even as law enforcement officers with agencies that seek out candidates with advanced degrees such as the Federal Bureau of Investigations (FBI). Attorneys working in criminal law must be comfortable with litigation (all prosecutors and criminal defense lawyers are trial lawyers), and must be thoroughly familiar with the rules of evidence and the rules of criminal procedure. In addition to knowing the criminal code, attorneys working in criminal law often work with scientific evidence (such as DNA evidence, blood testing, etc.), technical data (such as computer data encryption), financial records (banking, tax records, etc.), and various other issues from other fields that become significant in criminal cases. The work can be very rewarding at times, but it can also be stressful due to the high stakes involved in many cases. Criminal work can be distasteful when handling certain kinds of issues (rape, child pornography, etc.), but it can also be quite rewarding or even amusing at times.

Domestic Relations/Family Law

Domestic relations deals with issues related to the family, such as prenuptial (or antenuptial) agreements, marriage, divorce, civil unions, child custody and visitation, domestic violence, alimony, child support, adoption, and division of marital assets. Attorneys dealing with family law also need to have at least a basic familiarity with some of the overlapping issues in bankruptcy, pension and retirement, military law, criminal law (primarily domestic violence), jurisdiction, and conflict of laws, as these can have an impact on family court issues. A growing trend in family law is to send disputes to non-binding mediation to attempt to resolve disputes without a trial.

E-Commerce

A sub-specialty area of business law, computer law, and several other areas of practice, e-commerce deals specifically with issues that arise from conducting business over the internet. E-commerce can involve issues such as commercial and personal credit, electronic signatures, privacy and data protection, electronic contracts, spam and phishing, taxation, and intellectual property rights.

Election Law

Election law deals with the laws, rules, and regulations governing the election process. This can involve matters such as campaign finance, voting rights, voter identification, election reform, redistricting, election challenges and recounts, political blogging, internal procedures of political parties, and voter-sponsored initiatives. For attorneys who are actively involved in politics, it can be valuable to have a working knowledge of election law.

Employment & Labor Law

In general, employment law deals with the relationship between the employer and the employee, while labor law deals with the relationship between the employer and the labor union. These areas of law are governed by both federal and state statutes, administrative agency regulations, and extensive judicial interpretation. Labor law focuses on issues as they relate to the employees as a group, such as the right to form a union, the right to strike, retirement, pensions, and collective bargaining. Employment law deals with more individualized issues, such as employment discrimination, workers' compensation, and unemployment compensation. Attorneys who handle these areas of practice will be required to conduct extensive research and to constantly monitor the ever-changing tangle of applicable statutes and regulations.

Entertainment Law

Sometimes considered to be one of the "fun" areas of law, entertainment law requires considerable skill at negotiation, extensive legal knowledge, and an eye for detail. A strong talent in contract law is valuable in this field of practice. Entertainment lawyers will deal with issues such as trademark, copyright, contract, finance, communications, intellectual property, and marketing. Transactions

21

involved in entertainment law usually involve significant financial issues.

Environmental Law

Environmental law deals with federal and state laws designed to protect the environment from public or private actions which would potentially harm ecosystems, to protect individuals from the harmful results of pollution and other damage to the environment, and to address the scope of certain private property rights. Attorneys who handle this area of practice must be particularly familiar with an extensive web of federal regulations, and also need to develop a competency with subjects in the fields of biology, ecology, and toxicology.

Estate Planning

Estate planning is the process used by an individual or family to pass assets from one generation to the next. Practice in this area requires a familiarity with federal and state tax issues, as well as with probate law and practice. While basic estates may be limited to the drafting of simple wills, complicated estates (dealing with large sums of money) will likely involve the creation of various forms of trusts, gift planning, and other steps to maximize the amount of wealth passed from one generation to the next. It may also involve steps taken to protect beneficiaries from their own financial recklessness, such as placing the assets under the control of a trustee who controls how much of the estate is given to the beneficiary at any given time.

Foreign/Offshore Investments

Attorneys handling offshore investment issues should be well-versed in a number of areas of the law. International law, taxation, commercial and banking law, criminal law, the Patriot Act and other anti-terrorism legislation, securities, business law, and many other areas of practice are involved when an attorney seeks to handle offshore corporations and investments. This is an area that is generally reserved as a sub-specialty of tax law, and should not be undertaken without extensive research and training.

Government Contracts

Attorneys handling government contracts generally operate under a hybrid of contract law and administrative law. Government contracts are highly regulated to prevent misappropriation of funds, and disputes involving government contracts are controlled by specific procedures. The General Services Administration is responsible for enacting the regulations controlling contracts with the federal government.

Health Care

Health care law primarily involves aspects of administrative law, contract law, tort law, and insurance law. At the federal level, much of health care law revolves around the services and regulations of the Department of Health and Human Services. At the state level, issues related to insurance, health maintenance organizations (HMO's), and torts related to negligence and malpractice often arise. Attorneys working in health care will often be involved in matters related to medicare and medicaid, medical regulatory compliance, and insurance claims.

Immigration

Federal law governs the immigration process and most of the issues which fall within the gambit of immigration law. In general, immigration law determines who may enter the country, how long they may remain, what rights they have when they are here, and how they may become a permanent resident or full citizen. It also deals with those who have entered the country illegally, those who have entered legally but have stayed longer than authorized, and those who have engaged in conduct which requires their deportation (such as the commission of a violent felony). Attorneys are often employed to assist individuals who are seeking to legally navigate through the visa process to enter or remain in this country, to attempt to block deportation or obtain amnesty for certain individuals, and to represent employers facing prosecution for hiring illegal aliens.

Insurance

Insurance law includes many insurance issues that arise in health care law, but also expands more broadly to deal with the full range of insurance coverage. Issues may include property damage, lost income, physical impairment, emotional distress, and various other losses which may fall under some policy of insurance. In general, insurance is designed to shift risk from the individual to a group, in exchange for a premium. Insurance law typically becomes an issue when a dispute over coverage arises, and decisions regarding coverage will be significantly controlled by the precise wording of the insurance policy. Issues regarding good faith, ambiguity, fraud, and economic valuation are often involved. In many insurance disputes, the issue is not over whether coverage exists, but over what is a fair dollar amount to compensate for the loss.

Intellectual Property

Intellectual property deals with the kinds of property rights and protections that can be secured under federal law. Most issues deal with patents, copyrights, and trademarks. A patent is a right, created by the government, that excludes others from making, using, or selling the invention covered in the patent without the permission of the patent holder. It covers new inventions as well as improvements to existing inventions. A copyright provides the government's protection to published and unpublished "original works of authorship," which includes literary, musical, dramatic, artistic, and other intellectual works. Trademarks include any word, symbol, name, device, or combination thereof, intended to identify goods and distinguish them from the goods of others. The practice of intellectual property law often involves securing the applicable patents, copyrights, and/or trademarks, licensing rights, and dealing with disputes over whether certain usages infringe on the rights of others. Many disputes arise over the intellectual property rights involved in software development and medical research, where teams of people or groups may be involved in the work. A background in engineering or a closely related field is particularly valuable in the practice of most areas of intellectual property law.

International Law

International law consists of two overlapping areas of law: public international law and private international law. Public international law deals with rights between nations and the citizens of those nations, whereas private international law deals with transactions or disputes between private individuals involving issues related to more than one nation. Attorneys practicing these areas of law need to be familiar with international treaties, as well as the laws of the nations involved in the dispute. Fluency in foreign languages is a highly marketable skill in this area of practice.

Land Use Planning

Land use planning can involve federal, state, and local laws, and additionally can involve private land use restrictions (such as the regulations of a homeowner's association). While primarily a niche of real estate law, land use planning also involves areas such as administrative law, environmental law, and contract law. Attorneys involved in land use planning are often employed by contractors seeking to develop land, or by local governments who are regulating and overseeing the development. Issues may arise dealing with the Environmental Protection Agency (E.P.A.) or the Army Corp of Engineers, and often attorneys involved in land use planning will make appearances before county commissions, city councils, and local courts.

Legislation & Lobbying

A lobbyist is the representative of a group, business, organization, or other form of association attempting to influence the legislative process. While one does not have to be a lawyer to gain employment as a lobbyist, a legal background can be very useful. Working as a lobbyist involves advocating for the passage of certain legislation, attempting to block passage of other legislation, pushing for amendments to proposed or existing legislation, and also often involves attempting to sway public opinion as an indirect way to pressure the legislative process.

Military Law

Most attorneys who practice military law are current or former officers in the Judge Advocate General (JAG) Corps, or at least have a background in the military. The conduct of persons in the armed services is governed primarily by federal law and regulations, though state law can come into play at certain times. The primary body of military law is contained in the Uniform Code of Military Justice. Attorneys interested in military law should consider enlisting in the JAG Corps for some period of time prior to attempting to provide representation to individuals in this specialized area of practice.

Municipal Law

Attorneys who handle municipal law either represent municipalities, or they represent those who present claims to or against the municipal authority. Representing a municipality may include drafting or interpreting municipal ordinances, issues in municipal elections, zoning, contracts, and defending claims against the city. Those who represent private individuals, businesses, or groups in matters presented to or against the city commonly handle claims involving land use and development, appeals of property tax assessments, environmental issues, and business licensing and regulation.

Natural Resources

Closely tied to environmental law and often considered a sub-specialty, natural resources law deals with land, fish, wildlife, biota, air, water, ground water, drinking water supplies, and other such resources which are under the control of the federal or state government. Attorneys handling issues in this area will deal with environmental law, real estate, contracts, administrative law, and sometimes international law.

Personal Injury

Personal injury is a category of tort law dealing with cases in which an individual has suffered physical harm. The best known example of a personal injury claim is in automobile accident litigation, but these claims also arise as a result of products liability, medical malpractice, assault, toxic waste disposal, and any other scenario in which a person's claim revolves around physical harm. From the plaintiff's side, these cases are typically (but not always) handled on a contingent fee basis where the attorney receives a percentage of the amount recovered on behalf of the client. From the defendant's side, such cases are typically defendant on an hourly fee basis, though a defendant may be a counter-plaintiff or counter-claimant in certain cases. For example, if two cars are involved in an accident, both parties are injured, and each party blames the other for the accident, then both sides may assert liability claims.

Products Liability

Products liability is a form of tort law claim involving damage caused by a product. Liability may be passed along to one or several parties along the chain of production and distribution, depending on the specifics of the case. In order to succeed on a products liability claim, an attorney must be able to prove that a product was defective. Establishing this proof will typically involve the use of expert witnesses with relevant education, training, and/or experience. Additional steps in presenting a products liability case will vary from state to state. Products liability claims involve a significant commitment of time and of financial resources, and require a considerable degree of experience as a trial lawyer in order to present the case successfully.

Real Estate

Also known as real property or land law, real estate law deals with the right to use, control, and dispose of land. It generally refers to permanent structures above or below the land, as well as minerals, water, oil, gas, etc. Real estate law is governed almost exclusively by state law, though federal law can become involved with matters such as environmental claims. Real estate attorneys deal with the lease or transfer of real property, easements, boundary line disputes, zoning regulations, restrictive covenants, and at times issues such as natural resources or the environment.

Secured Transactions

Secured transactions law is a specialty which encompasses aspects of banking law, bankruptcy, business law, and contracts. Secured transactions are regulated by each state under their applicable version of Article 9 of the Uniform Commercial Code. In a secured transaction, a lender (known as the secured party) loans money to a debtor in exchange for a security interest in some form of collateral provided by the debtor. If the debtor fails to pay the loan according to its terms, then the secured party has the right to take possession of the collateral. In some situations, this right to take possession of the collateral may apply even if the debtor files bankruptcy, though such a step would require approval by a bankruptcy court.

Securities

Securities law deals with the rights of investors to receive accurate information about the investments they make in the marketplace. Federal and state law both regulate the securities market, and focus primarily on the market for common stocks. The Securities Exchange Commission oversees and regulates securities issues which fall under federal law.

Sports Law

Sports law requires skill at contract law, but also requires the attorney to be knowledgeable about tort issues and antitrust law. An attorney whose practice involves sports law often will be involved with the relationship between the athlete and the team owner. Such involvement will often lead to representation in matters related to product or event endorsements as well.

Tax Law

Also known as income tax law, tax law deals with the obligation of individuals, corporations, and other organizations to pay a portion of their income to the government. Some states do not have an income tax, but the federal income tax applies nationwide. Tax attorneys often have backgrounds in accounting, and many go on to obtain an advanced degree in tax law. They often represent clients in disputes with the Internal Revenue Service or state taxing authorities, and they are usually involved in estate planning for wealthy individuals.

Tort Law

Tort law is a very broad category which deals with the right to litigate civil wrongs, and deal with allegations of injury or harm in some manner. Under tort law, a party may sue another party for monetary compensation for the wrong committed, and may request an injunction to stop current conduct or prevent existing conduct. In general, tort claims may be categorized as intentional torts (such as assault), negligent torts (such as a car accident), or strict liability torts (such as the manufacture of a defective product). Often more than one type of tort claim is alleged when litigation is commenced. Most standard tort claims fall under state law, but there are many situations where federal issues or federal jurisdiction may apply.

Transportation

Often overlapping with aviation and admiralty law, transportation law is the specialization which deals with the moving of goods from one place to another. Attorneys working in transportation must be familiar with regulations issued by the federal Department of Transportation, as well as by similar state agencies. Issues in transportation law commonly involve the transportation of good by railway systems or by use of the interstate highway system.

Workers Compensation

Workers compensation, also known as workmans compensation, is a system of laws designed to ensure that employees who are injured on the job receive financial support and compensation without the need of litigation. State law typically establishes tables and schedules for determining the amount of compensation an employee should receive as a temporary benefit while recovering from an on-the-job injury, and will also provide a means for determining an amount of compensation for permanent injuries. Non-military federal employees receive a similar benefit from the federal government under the Federal Employment Compensation Act. Other federal legislation also exists for certain specific categories of workers as well. Litigation under worker's compensation laws often centers around disputes over whether a person's injury is an on-the-job injury, whether the individual is an employee or an independent contractor, whether the person's injury is as severe as the person claims, whether the person has been wrongfully discharged for filing a worker's compensation claim, and determining the percentage of permanent impairment.

CHAPTER THREE

Selecting An Office Location

An important decision affecting the future of your law practice is the issue of location. Where you choose to locate your office will have a significant impact on the initial clientele who contact you for representation. For example, if your office is located in an economically depressed area, your clientele will most likely consist of those in the community in need of low-priced legal services. If your office is in a high-rise office suite in a downtown area, your clientele are more likely to be among the more affluent members of the business community. If you are located in an area with a high concentration of senior adults, expect your practice to consist of a significant amount of basic estate planning and elder law. If you are near the courthouse, you can anticipate being approached to handle various forms of litigation[3]. Do not take these statements as absolutes, but rather as over-generalized statements of the trends you can expect to see in certain locations. As your practice and reputation grows, your name will become a more significant factor than your location in who chooses to hire you. But when you are first starting out, the location of your office will create certain predictable trends in your client traffic.

---

[3] As amazing as it may seem, many people do not try to retain a lawyer until after the first time they have to make an appearance in court on their case. They walk out of the courthouse with the realization that they are facing a situation they cannot handle on their own, and start looking around for an attorney.

Professional Image

The location of your practice creates an initial image of your practice. When you are first starting out, you do not have the luxury of a reputation to draw in clients. Instead, you must create an appearance of professionalism and competence, and begin to make yourself known in the community. As superficial as it may seem, the street address of your office can be a significant factor in that public perception of you and your abilities. After all, if you needed heart surgery, would you seek out the new doctor in town with an office behind the meat packing plant? Or would you contact the physician in a professional district who meets patients in a more professional setting? Appearances are not everything, but they are important in building a new law practice.

While location and appearance are important, do not become carried away with the idea of a luxurious office space. You are looking for something that makes you look like a professional, not like a millionaire. And, if you get evicted from your office two months after moving in because you are unable to pay the rent, you will not make a good impression on anybody. Look to balance professionalism with affordability in selecting your office space.

Accessibility & Convenience

Another factor to consider in choosing a location is accessibility and convenience, both for yourself and for your clients. The longer you practice law, the more important this factor will become to you. Is it more convenient for your practice to be close to (or at) home, or is it better to be near the courthouse? If your practice will consist primarily of matters such as drafting contracts and deeds, forming corporations, or planning estates, then you will have little need to be near the courthouse. In that situation, an office close to home makes more sense. And persons seeking those legal services may be more likely to contact your office if you are located closer to their residential communities. On the other hand, if your practice will involve a significant amount of litigation, then it can be wise to locate your office within walking distance or a short drive from the courthouse. The amount of time you spend commuting will add up very quickly.

Law Office Suite

One good option for a new attorney is to locate his or her office in a suite or building where a number of attorneys are in practice. This could be a cost-sharing arrangement with other attorneys, such as sharing a receptionist, photocopier, etc., or it could simply be getting an office in a building where a number of attorneys have their offices. When I first started my practice, I was in a small two-story office building shared by about a half-dozen attorneys and a few other professional business offices. The only shared expense was a receptionist downstairs at the front door, who would answer the phones and notify any office when one of their clients came in the door. The use of a large conference room in the building was included in the rental of office space. Other attorneys have great success in reducing their overhead expenses by sharing even more expenses, without forming a firm and without sharing income, by sharing office equipment, secretarial time, and other easily divisible expenses.

Some attorneys are hesitant about being in close proximity to other law offices due to a fear that the other attorneys will be a drain on business. However, the opposite result is more likely, since the new attorney will have very little business for anyone to drain away in the first place. What the new lawyer needs more than anything is referrals from other lawyers. Being down the hall from other attorneys is one of the best ways to start a referral network, because you will be building personal relationships with experienced lawyers who can send you cases they do not want or are unable to take for some reason. Also, it is quite common for someone to go see an experienced attorney, and be quoted a fee that is simply beyond their price range. They walk out of that attorney's office shaking their heads and wondering what to do, and then they spot your office. Many new attorneys make a living being retained by clients who simply could not afford their first choice of attorney[4]. Being a new lawyer, your fees are almost certainly going to be lower than the experienced attorneys, and you are probably in a position to devote more time to their case as well. Proximity to other lawyers puts you in a position to gain more clients than you could otherwise gain with your

---

[4] Some attorneys jokingly refer to this method of obtaining clients as "picking up scraps" or "eating leftovers."

non-existent reputations.

Experienced attorneys often have clients or potential clients who come to them for matters which they do not handle, or which are not worth their time to handle due to economic issues or time constraints. The attorney may simply be too busy at that moment to take on a client who has an urgent and time-consuming need, or perhaps the attorney has some conflict of interest that prevents him or her from handling the case. Rather than simply brushing off a person who contacted them for representation, most attorneys will make a referral to another attorney that they believe may be interested in the case. If your office is mere footsteps away, and you have developed a good relationship with that attorney, you could start your practice just by picking up referrals off of the other attorneys.

When I first started my practice, one of the attorneys down the hall from me was approached by one of his former clients about resolving a minor real estate issue. He did not have the time or inclination to bother with her problem, so he referred her case to me. Being a brand new lawyer, I had the time and inclination to work for anyone who could pay me a small fee, which she did. I succeeded in accomplishing everything she requested I do for her, and did so within a relatively short period of time. A year later, when she was involved in a crippling accident involving both employer negligence and a defective product, she called me instead of her old attorney. Though the case was beyond my new-attorney budget or experience to handle, I made a referral to an experienced products liability specialist who eventually sent me a six-figure referral fee. This boost to my practice happened entirely because the other attorney was too busy to handle her previous small case when she needed him. People often choose an attorney for their big case simply because that attorney did a good job for them on a small matter in the past.

Another important benefit of being located near other attorneys is the wealth of experience it puts at your disposal. Most attorneys in solo practice tend to be quite congenial with new attorneys, and generally will be willing to provide you with advice on your practice. During the early days of my practice, the attorney-friendships I made were a critical element in my success because of the practical advice they were willing to share with me. Without their help, there were many times where I would have been completely lost.

In addition to providing practical advice, attorneys who are in close proximity to you can be a great source of legal forms. With the growth of the internet and the ready availability of legal resources, the need to go to other attorneys for basic documents has diminished to some degree. However, there are many needs that will arise in your practice that simply cannot be satisfied by an internet search for legal forms. Most local court systems have rules for local practice, and a local attorney can help you understand what works with one judge but not with another. When dealing with the court system in your area, the best source for forms is usually local.

Private Office Space

Some attorneys choose to have their own office building away from other lawyers. Often they will find an older house along a major roadway and establish an office there. While this will deprive the new attorney of the convenience of stepping across the hallway to ask an experienced attorney for advice, it does allow more freedom for practice placement. For example, if your practice is situated close to a school where a number of parents drive by every day, finding ways to target the legal needs of that demographic (such as family or education law) could be profitable.

If you choose to establish a practice in a location separated from other attorneys, it is still very important that you take steps to develop relationships with other attorneys in your community. Attend bar meetings and functions, get to know other attorneys in the courtroom during motion dockets, join internet discussion groups, and try to find attorneys who do not mind advising you from time to time. An attorney in a building or office with other attorneys should take these steps as part of developing his or her practice, but it is absolutely essential to learning to practice law if your practice is physically isolated from that of other attorneys. After all, are you more likely to loan your lawnmower to the new neighbor that moved in next door, or to the stranger who has moved in across town?

After several years of practicing in a building with numerous other attorneys, I leased a building on one of the major roads through town. Day and night, there is a constant flow of traffic past the office, and every person driving by sees my office sign. They may not necessarily pay any attention to the sign, but by seeing it over and over it puts the name into their minds. This is one of many simple ways that an attorney can build name recognition in a community.

It is not uncommon for people to come in to see me simply because they have been driving past my office every day, and finally had a need for my services. This seems to be especially common with the walk-in clients.[5] Most of the time the walk-ins of this nature have been people who "just want to ask a question," but on several occasions those quick questions have turned into large fees.

The Home Office

Many attorneys choose to start their practice from a home office. This is certainly the most economical way to open a practice, though it carries a number of risks. Allowing clients to come to your home for appointments opens up the risk of an angry or mentally ill client showing up at your door in the middle of the night or on a Sunday afternoon when you are trying to relax. This can be particularly problematic if you have young children in your household.

There are many good, stable, honest, and trustworthy people who will be your clients, who would never abuse the privilege of knowing the location of your home. However, as a general rule, the clients you would least want to have access to you outside of work will be the very ones who feel free to come by your house any time they have a question or

---

[5] Walk-in clients are those who do not schedule an appointment, but simply walk in asking to see you.

complaint. When possible, take steps to guard your privacy, such as arranging the use of a conference room for meeting with clients you would not want in your home.

I would also recommend having an unpublished home phone number, even if your office is in your house. Before getting an unpublished home number, I often received calls from clients who thought their situation was an "emergency," but whose problem could have waited until the morning. As a practical matter, there are few things an attorney can do to help a client in the middle of the night. I also received calls from clients who simply wanted to check on the status of their case, or to pick up some "free" advice because some random legal question had come up while drinking beer with a buddy. While some attorneys may be comfortable with 24-hour availability, I need a break from work when I leave the office. You will find that you can perform better work for your clients if you make sure to get a break from them to rest and recharge.

If you are concerned about making sure clients can reach you in a true emergency, hire an answering service to answer your calls after hours. If there is a true emergency, they can call you to relay the message, and you can then decide whether it is necessary to return the call at that time. Many people, upon reaching an answering service, will simply leave a message for you to call. Thus, it serves as a good filter so that you are only disturbed at times when there is actually a situation that requires your immediate attention. Nonetheless, if your office is at home, you can keep an eye on emergencies by simply checking your voice mail from time to time during the hours your office is closed.

Starting a practice from home can be very economically efficient, as well as being the ultimate in convenience. It can be great to walk into your office at any time you wish, day or night. If you are having trouble sleeping, for example, you can walk into your home office and work on a file that is on your mind. The night before a trial, you have easy access to any of the materials relevant to your case. You have tremendous savings in office rental, gas costs, and the other expenses of operating a separate business. And, you can take certain deductions from your taxes for the portion of your home dedicated exclusively to the operation of your business.

Whether to work at home is a personal decision that may dictated by the nature of your practice. If your practice will consist primarily of appellate work, for example, then there is almost no need for meeting with clients in the first place. However, if you intend to handle criminal defense or family law, a large degree of client contact is necessary. As a general rule, the more contact you need to have with your clients, the more need there is to have a separate physical office.

The Virtual Office

Some attorneys are moving away from the traditional method of operating an office, and developing a "virtual office" instead. This involves running most aspects of a law practice from a phone (or cell phone) and a computer (preferably notebook). Sometimes this is done from a home office, and other times it is done through an arrangement among attorneys to share a receptionist and/or a conference room, but with very little else in the way of an actual office.

A receptionist can answer the calls and then forward them through to your cell phone, or you may choose to answer the phone yourself. Meetings with clients can be held in the conference room (coordinated with the schedules of other attorneys using the space) or sometimes even at the offices of clients. Clients can also communicate with you by email, which enables you to provide them information quickly without being tied up on the phone.

The virtual office is the ultimate in economic efficiency, and operating this way is becoming a growing trend among experienced attorneys. The majority of an attorney's work is done outside of the client's presence, so why does it matter whether the attorney is in an expensive office or is sitting on the sofa in his living room? If your practice will involve areas that do not require much "face time" with clients, then this is an option for the new lawyer to consider seriously. This kind of practice would not have been realistic thirty years ago, but modern technology has made it a very convenient option.

The major problems with this approach are that it can create some difficulties with scheduling meetings with clients, it can make it more complicated when clients are trying to drop off payments to you, it deprives you of the "free advertising" that comes from a physical office, and it can create the impression to some that you cannot afford an office like other attorneys (which, in the new lawyer's case, may be true).

The most potentially damaging of these problems is the last one, because an attorney's reputation and image have a tremendous impact on whether or not someone chooses to hire that person. If a person believes that an attorney is struggling financially, they may be reluctant to hire him or her for representation. However, an effective way to deal with this issue is to turn it into a positive attribute. When this issue over the lack of a physical office arises, the best way to deal with it is to explain that by having such low overhead, you are able to charge lower fees to your clients. If you were paying for an expensive office to sit in and paying a receptionist to answer your phone, then you would have to raise your rates. By running a virtual office, you can provide your services more economically to your clients.

If you have worked out an arrangement for the use of a conference room for meeting with clients, or even have a small office space located somewhere, then many clients may never realize you are running your practice as a virtual office. After all, when a client calls on the phone, that client has no idea where you actually are when you answer it.

The concept of the virtual office has become so success-ful in the business world that there now exist companies who will serve as an office for you. They accept your mail deliveries; they can answer your phone and schedule your appointments; they provide you with a prestigious address; and they make this affordable by providing this service to numerous businesses and professionals at the same time. Facilities of this nature are becoming increasingly common in the bigger cities, and will likely expand into some of the smaller markets over time.

CHAPTER FOUR

Choosing A Form Of Business

An important task is to determine which form of business is the best choice for operating your law practice. Each state determines which specific forms of business are legally authorized, but these will all fall within certain general categories outlined below.

When setting up your business, obtain the services of a qualified accountant to assist you with your financial planning. One of your goals in choosing a form of business is to maximize your tax benefits. Each person's financial situation is different, and an accountant can provide guidance and suggestions that you never received in law school, particularly as it relates to taxation issues in your practice. The initial meeting with your accountant will be one of the most important steps in mapping the future of your business.

Corporations

A common form of business used by attorneys is the corporation. Incorporating your practice provides many benefits, such as avoiding self-employment tax, creating a distinction between the attorney's personal and work finances, and providing some level of liability protection from the actions of partners, associates, and employees. However, incorporation will not protect you from liability for your personal actions or your own professional negligence. Additionally, while you will be able to incur some debts solely in the name of the corporation (thus precluding personal liability), most creditors (banks, credit cards) will require you to sign onto the debt as a personal guarantor.

Most states provide members of certain professions with the option of forming a "professional corporation" (P.C.), so review your state law for details. Although a law practice can be incorporated and issue shares of stock, non-lawyers cannot be shareholders in a professional corporation. While you can accept loans from non-lawyers, you cannot give them an ownership stake in the firm.

One of the benefits of incorporation is the complete separation of personal finances from those of the business. It is much easier to keep track of your business income and expenses if everything flows through a corporate bank account. It is also easier to keep track of your personal income tax obligations, since you will be required to withhold taxes on yourself from your paychecks. You may also be able to receive a portion of your income as a stock dividend (since you own the stock of the corporation), which will be subject to less taxation than your salary. However, this should only be done with the guidance of an accountant, as there are certain limitations on how and to what extent this can be done. As a corporation, you may also have a broader range of options for setting up a retirement plan, medical insurance and reimbursement plan, etc.

Sole Proprietorship

Many attorneys in solo practice choose to operate as sole proprietors, avoiding the formalities of incorporation. This can be a relatively simple way to operate a business, though it can also create bookkeeping problems along the way. When income comes in, you may be able to give it to yourself directly, but you will be required to track and report your income and pay estimated taxes out of it on at least a quarterly basis. From a practical standpoint, it can be difficult to force yourself not to spend this large a portion of your income unless you have been keeping it set aside in a separate account. However, many attorneys see no need to go through the formalities of a corporation while in solo practice, and choose this simple and direct approach.

As a sole proprietorship, you are personally liable to all of your creditors, whether for professional services or for nonprofessional matters related to the operation of your business. There is no distinction between your personal and your professional finances, and you are fully liable for all debts of your business. Many creditors require a personal guarantee on all of your business debts anyway, even if you are incorporated or have formed a limited liability company. However, the lack of a business structure as a shield will leave you open to potential liabilities that would have otherwise only been chargeable to your business. For example, if your secretary is delivering paperwork for you during the course of her employment and is involved in a car accident, you are a potential defendant for her negligent driving. With a corporate shield, your personal assets would be safe. As a sole proprietor, you would be facing personal liability as the direct employer responsible for the employee's actions.

Partnership

Partnerships can be formed in a number of ways, and the options available will be determined by state law. Some partnerships are simply two or more sole practitioners operating an office together; others are more formal business structures that provide some degree of liability protection from the actions of the other partners. If you are considering going into partnership with another attorney, you should carefully review the various options under your state's laws and discuss the tax implications with your accountant. Most states offer options for general and limited partnerships, and your state law will determine the pros and cons of each.

Limited Liability Companies

Depending on the structure in your individual state, a limited liability company will be a hybrid between a corporation and a partnership or sole proprietorship. Often these will provide the liability protections of a corporation, but the tax benefits and convenience of a partnership or sole proprietorship. The owners of an LLC are called members, rather than partners or shareholders, and an LLC provides a very flexible system for distributing profits to those members. However, an LLC does not have the benefit of perpetual existence that a corporation provides, and is generally dissolved by the death or bankruptcy of a member. Thus, while it is very convenient for a solo attorney or a small partnership, it may not be a good choice if your plan is to eventually expand into a large firm. However, if you intend to remain solo or to only have one or two partners, it can be an excellent choice for simplifying your business operations.

CHAPTER FIVE

Setting Up A Business

There are a variety of steps you must take in order to set up your practice. Your accountant will provide significant guidance in this stage of the process. The following items are the essential issues you need to address.

Business Entity Formation

The previous chapter discussed choices available for forming a business entity for your law practice. You will need to go forward with formally creating the business entity you have chosen before you can take most of the following steps. For example, if you are corporation, at a minimum you will need to draft your Articles of Incorporation and record them with the appropriate governmental authorities. Most states require corporations and limited liability companies to register with that state's secretary of state, and often require registration with the local probate court as well.

Tax Identification Numbers

If an attorney chooses a form of business other than a sole proprietorship, then he or she must obtain a tax identification number for the business. The IRS has a simple, one-page application that you will need to complete to obtain your federal identification number. A federal tax identification number is available online for most forms of business at www.irs.gov, by sending in a written application, or by delegating the task to your accountant as part of his or her duties in helping start your business. You may need to obtain various identification numbers from your state, and possibly from your county and city depending on where you practice. Due to the complexity of the state and federal tax codes, and the various government agencies involved in taxing the operation of a business (such as payroll taxes, licenses, and unemployment), it is advisable to employ your accountant to handle these matters. Otherwise, you may neglect to register with an agency required for the operation of a business, or fail to understand the taxes and fees you are required to pay on a monthly, quarterly, and/or annual basis.

Business License

Once you have formed your business, you will need to obtain a business license. You will need a license either from your city or from your county, and in some places you will need both. A business license for operating a law practice is not difficult to obtain, and in most places is based on a minimum fee plus a fee based on your previous year's revenue. As a new business, you should only be expected to post the minimum assessment.

Federal Agencies and Courts

If you expect to handle cases before federal agencies, check with those agencies as to their registration requirements. Most will require the filing of a certificate, which is a relatively simple process with most agencies.

To appear in federal court, you must be a member of your state bar, and you must file a separate application to appear in that court. This is also a relatively simple process, as long as no major problems have developed since the time you made it past the Character and Fitness review by your state bar.

For certain courts, you may also need to complete an orientation or training course before handling cases. For example, many bankruptcy courts require attorneys to complete a brief training session on online filing and on local procedures before they can begin filing cases.

Liability Insurance

No business structure will protect you from personal liability for your own professional negligence. The best method for obtaining that protection is through the purchase of professional liability insurance. Ask other attorneys in your community for recommendations of companies or agents they would recommend, or contact your state bar association for a list of liability insurance companies in your state. You may be able to obtain a discount rate through your bar association, or through your membership in a professional association (ATLA, NACDL, etc.).

Many attorneys practice without insurance due to the high cost of premiums. While this is understandable, it also creates a risk of bankruptcy or severe personal financial damage if an aggrieved client makes a successful claim against you. A lack of liability insurance will also prevent you from being listed with many state and local lawyer referral services.

Some attorneys are of the opinion that carrying liability insurance actually increases the risk of being sued. Just as many attorneys will not pursue an auto accident claim against an uninsured driver, many will not bother to sue an attorney who does not have insurance to pay a settlement or judgment.

In addition to providing liability protection, most liability companies sponsor seminars and publish newsletters on topics that will assist you in avoiding ethical and professional problems. The seminars can be particularly valuable, as they are usually free and will count towards your state's continuing legal education requirements.

While the cost of insurance may appear prohibitive, consider the balancing of that cost with things like the savings on continuing legal education and the income benefit of referrals from lawyer referral services. One good referral could cover the cost of the insurance in itself.

Bank Accounts

Your practice will need at least two bank accounts for the operation of your business, and you may want to consider having additional accounts as discussed below. If you are using a form of business other than a sole proprietorship, then you will need your tax identification number and your incorporation or organization paperwork to open the account.

1. Operating Account

The first account that must be opened is a general business operating account. This account will be used for depositing income and paying expenses. You can also obtain a debit/credit card to use on this account for purchases made online, or for times when you may not wish to use a check (such as a business dinner).

The most reliable way to keep track of your exact income and expenses is to run everything through this operating account. This way, even if your records are somehow destroyed (fire, hurricane, etc. - yes, it happens), you could still access the bank records and reconstruct your previous year for filing your taxes. It also helps you have a clear view of how much you are earning and spending when your monthly bank statement arrives, and you see the totals in each category.

2. *Trust Account*

The second account you must open is an escrow or trust account. This will be for handling money that belongs to clients as part of some legal transaction (real estate sale, personal injury settlement, litigation expenses, etc.), and also for holding fees that you have not yet billed against a client retainer.

In most states, your trust account must be authorized by the state bar association, and the bank may be required to report misconduct on the account (primarily bounced checks) to the state bar. You may need a letter from your state bar association authorizing you to open the account prior to setting it up at the bank. Lawyers' trust accounts are a very serious matter, and they are not to be mishandled under any circumstances. Never withdraw fees you have not yet earned; never "borrow" a client's money to pay your bills; never lose track of which money belongs to which client. While your state bar association may be helpful to you with some problems that arise in your life, they generally show no mercy or sympathy for abuses of a trust account. It is not your money to misuse.

3. Payroll Account (Optional)

If you are not using a payroll service to handle paying your self and others in your firm, then it may be advisable to obtain an additional account for handling payroll and setting aside payroll taxes. It is much easier to set that money aside now than it is to come up with it all at once later. The IRS considers payroll taxes to be similar to money you have set aside in your trust account, and may even be able to assess personal liability against you for unpaid corporate payroll taxes. In some situations, it can even result in criminal prosecution. Treat payroll withholding taxes carefully, set the money aside as you go, and pay it on time. Your accountant can assist you with making sure your payments are timely and accurate.

4. Savings Account (optional).

A wise practice for attorneys is to open a savings account of some kind, whether it is a traditional bank account, money market account, or some other method for setting money aside into an interest bearing account. One of your goals in building your practice should be to set aside enough money to where you could operate your business for three to six months with little or no income. Preferably, of course, you have done this before starting your practice, but that bankroll may become depleted while you are getting on your feet. As soon as possible, you need to replenish (or create) those funds to provide you with a security net in the event that your practice falls upon hard times. Remember, just setting aside a small portion of your income every month can make a big difference down the road when you hit a bad month and do not make enough to meet your income requirements.

Telephone & Internet

It is very likely that the most memorable phone numbers have already been taken by other businesses. However, it never hurts to ask your phone company for your preferred number, or for something that will be easy to remember (1111, 1234, etc.).

When first starting out, you will need to look at obtaining at least one phone line for business calls (more if you have a secretary or partners), and another line which can serve as a dedicated fax line. The fax line can also serve as a DSL or other high-speed internet connection, without either function interfering with the other.

While it was not necessary in the past, now it is almost essential that you have internet access, including email, at your office. Many court systems are already on a system of electronic filing, and the rest will get there eventually. Clients often desire to communicate by email, and in fact having a website with an email link can generate potential client inquiries that can lead to new business.

Most telephone companies will offer some kind of business package, which may include phone, fax, internet, long distance, and other services at a discounted rate. You may be eligible for certain discounts on long distance through your bar membership or a professional association. Check with your state bar association, your professional associations, and long distance companies which are independent of your local phone service before selecting a plan.

Notary

If you hire a secretary, you need to go through the process of getting him or her a notary seal for your state. It is very common for certain legal documents to need a notary seal, and you do not want to be sending clients to other offices to get their signatures notarized.

If you do not have a secretary or do not plan to hire one right away, then you will need to become a notary yourself. For the most part, there is no problem with an attorney serving as the notary for most documents he or she has prepared. However, if a secretary or paralegal in your office is available as a notary, then have that person serve as the notary for your documents instead.

Remember that a notarization is more significant than merely witnessing a signature. A notary seal is a sign that the notary has, among other things, confirmed the identity of the person signing the document. Merely asking someone their name is not sufficient for this purpose, and a notary can be held liable for notarizing a signature that was actually forged.

Employee Issues

If you will have employees, there are several forms that must be completed and there are certain documents you must obtain from your employee. The forms generally required by the federal government are the I-9 and the W-4. Form I-9 is the Employment Eligibility Verification, which requires you to verify that your employee is eligible to work in the United States. Form W-4 is the Employee's Withholding Allowance Certificate, which is used to determine the amount of income tax to withhold from your employee's wages. Other forms may apply to your particular employee's situation, so make sure to review these matters with your accountant.

In addition to the federal documentation, most states will have similar form requirements to handle state income tax (if applicable). Check with your accountant and/or your state government to ensure that you have met all of your state's requirements.

CHAPTER SIX

Office Furniture, Equipment, and Supplies

There are certain "tools of the trade" that you need to practice law. While not all of the items discussed in this chapter are absolutely essential, they will certainly make your life much easier without breaking your budget.

Buying vs Renting

There are some who encourage the idea of renting furniture rather than purchasing it outright. The major advantage of this, of course, is that you could furnish your office with nicer furniture than you can actually afford to purchase. On the other hand, this means making payments every month for items that you may never actually own, or that will ultimately cost you more than they are worth.

I believe very strongly in having as little debt as possible, and paying off existing debt as quickly as possible. Purchasing less expensive furniture that you then own forever is a much better investment than furnishing your office with leased furniture that you could lose if business goes flat.

Do not live beyond your means in furnishing your law office. Get what you need, at a price you can afford. You do not want to appear cheap or broke, but there is no point in unnecessary opulence either. When you become more wealthy later, then you can look at buying more expensive furnishings. And by that time, you will not care that much about the furniture. New lawyers seem to be more concerned about things like new furniture than the older lawyers are. No one cares if the old attorney has an old desk, so why do you think they will care if yours has a few years on it too?

Office Furniture

To properly furnish your office, you need to obtain the following items:

1. Desk

Everyone expects their attorney to be sitting behind a "lawyer's desk." It is not essential that it be the most luxurious desk in the world. However, you should invest in something that is at least one step above particle board. A nice desk portrays an image of professionalism, and will not break your budget as much as you might expect.

While it may be tempting to purchase new, beautiful furniture, a good way to acquire better furniture for a lower price is to purchase a second-hand desk. The easiest way to do this (apart from knowing someone who is selling one) is to go to an office furniture store and ask to see the used furniture in their warehouse. Many office furniture stores have a large selection of old furniture that they have acquired as trade-ins, at estate sales, or simply by customers asking them to haul something off when a new purchase was delivered. The desk in my office today was purchased for less than half of its retail price, because I purchased it used from a furniture store. By making the purchase this way, I was able to acquire a desk that is much nicer than what I could have otherwise afforded at the time. And while at one time I would have liked a more expensive desk, now I am completely happy with the one I have and see an upgrade as a waste of money.

2. Secretarial desk

Your secretary (when you get one) is most likely going to need a larger work space than you will need. Do not even consider getting a standard sized desk for her - unless you plan to get her two or three of them. Many office supply stores sell great secretarial desks that are either a two-desk setup, or which are set up as a credenza with an L-shaped design. The L-shaped design is particularly useful and efficient - unless you plan to try to move it around frequently, at which time it becomes a big hassle.

3. Chairs

Chairs can be surprisingly expensive. You need to look at three kinds of chairs: your chair, your secretary's chair, and chairs for your clients.

For your personal chair, you need to balance style, comfort, and cost. When first starting out, there is no need for you to purchase an expensive chair to try to impress people. Most of them will not really pay that much attention to your chair, unless it is obviously cheap or obviously expensive. Try to find a large chair, with a swivel base and which enables you to lean back. You will be spending a lot of time sitting in that chair, and you need to make sure you are comfortable. If you are not comfortable sitting in a chair for two minutes in the store, imagine how bad it would feel to sit in it all day long. A comfortable chair will make it much easier for you to work the long hours ahead of you. Your best choice would be to find a chair with a modern ergonomic design.

For your secretary's chair, you need to consider many of the same issues in selecting your chair, but the typical style of a secretary's chair is different than that of the attorney. For your secretary, the appearance of the chair is really not that important. Any secretary who spends all day typing on a computer will tell you that what they really want is a comfortable chair that is ergonomically designed for comfort in doing the job. Someone who spends most of the day hunched over a computer is looking for comfort more than style. Most chairs of this nature can be purchased at a reasonable price, and many new attorneys use the same chairs for themselves simply because of the cost savings and the level of comfort they provide.

For client chairs, you should look for something that looks reasonably professional, but nothing more. Your clients do not need to sit in expensive leather wingback chairs, unless you just have an obsessive need to impress people with your furniture. And in fact, those elaborate chairs are usually less comfortable than something more basic. A simple chair with a cushioned seat and back can look professional, and will get the job done at a minimal cost. If you wish to upgrade later, then certainly do so, but for the beginning attorney there is no reason to purchase expensive chairs. You will need several of these chairs for your lobby and/or secretarial area, and two or three more for meetings in your personal office.

4. Book cases

You are a lawyer, and clients expect you to have books in your office. It does not matter that you are doing all of your research online, or that you purchase all of your books on CD-ROM. The fact remains that you will look odd if you do not have law books around you.

If you are not in a position to start building a "real" legal library, just put up an inexpensive bookshelf and cover it with books from law school. Most of those books are so thick that it only takes a few of them to fill up a shelf. After three years of law school, you have acquired a lot of material that you will never read again. Nonetheless, put it on a shelf, so that clients will glance at it and think you are knowledgeable. As an added advantage, this reduces the need to fill empty spaces along the walls. Just throw up a bookcase, fill it with old law books, and your basic office decoration is done. You can buy new books later when you figure out which ones you really need.

You can find very reasonably priced bookcases without even going to an office supply store. Any store that carries hardware and building supplies will usually have a section with various kinds of furniture that only needs basic assembly. By simply being willing to tighten a few screws and assemble a few parts, you can have a nice bookcase without spending a lot of money. While you need a bookcase in your office, there is no reason to invest a large amount of money into it.

5. *Filing cabinets*

Filing cabinets are a necessity, at least for your active files. Older files can be safely stored in boxes once you are done with them, but you need to have quick and easy access to the files you are currently handling.

Filing cabinets are primarily for function, not for appearance. There is really no reason to buy an expensive set of filing cabinets when a cheap one will do the job just as well. Clients do not expect you to have mahogany filing cabinets; a traditional metal one will do just fine.

An issue that arises in law practice management is over whether to use legal sized or letter sized files. This issue, of course, dictates what size filing cabinets you will need. While there was a time when legal sized files would have been standard, they are now rarely used. Almost everything you do in your law practice will be on letter size paper, and anything larger (such as a deed) can simply be folded to fit when necessary. There is no reason to purchase legal size filing cabinets (which are more expensive) and legal size file folders (also more expensive), when you are going to be wasting that space. Over time, you will save a lot of money by going with the smaller sized folders. At your startup, you will save money as well as space by basing everything around letter sized documents.

6. *Plants*

It may not seem important, but keeping living things in your office is good for your health. It creates a more peaceful atmosphere for your clients, who come to your office feeling anxious. Anything you can do to make your clients feel relaxed in your office is a good investment, particularly when it is as inexpensive as setting out a few plants.

Most plants are not very expensive. With a little care, they will fill your office with beauty and tranquility. They are good for filling spaces that would otherwise be empty in your office. And if you are taking good care of your plants, it will send a subconscious message to your clients that you will take care of them too.

7. Coffee table/end table

When clients are waiting to see you, they need something to do. Even if they cannot read, they will pick up a magazine and look through it while they wait. A coffee table simply functions as a place to put things you want clients to read, whether that be pamphlets, flyers, or simply magazines. It also serves well as a place to put promotional items you would like the clients to take with them when they leave. For example, I order pens that have been imprinted with my name, my practice name, and the address and phone number of my office. I keep a supply of them in a cup on my coffee table. Every few days, I have to fill the cup again because so many people take them. You could also keep a firm brochure on the coffee table, or perhaps copies of an article where you were profiled in the newspaper in relation to some major case.

One point to keep in mind in selecting reading material for the coffee table is to make sure the material is appropriate. For example, while you may enjoy reading "adult" magazines every month, you should think carefully before leaving them sitting on your coffee table for clients to peruse. A copy of Time or Newsweek would be much more appropriate.

8. Wastebaskets

You need a wastebasket in every room. And you should always keep trash bags in those wastebaskets. Do not bother getting something expensive or fancy just because you think it might look more professional or classy. A simple plastic container for your trash is all that you need and is all that people expect.

9. Lamps

Lamps are only necessary if you do not have adequate overhead lighting. If you need additional lighting for your office, a simple lamp on your desk will usually suffice.

Office Equipment

In selecting office equipment, keep two things in mind. You do not want to purchase outdated equipment that will need frequent repairs and that may cause difficulties in finding replacement parts. You also do not need the latest, greatest, and most expensive new equipment on the market either. At this stage of your practice, your needs are going to be relatively simple. Purchase equipment that is good enough to get the job done for now, and keep yourself on a tight budget. You can upgrade later when you actually have an income again.

Also keep in mind that you can cut some of the following expenses by combining some pieces of equipment into one. An example of this is the combination of a printer, fax machine, scanner, and photocopier into one piece of equipment. This can provide substantial savings over the old way of purchasing each of these items of equipment individually.

1. Photocopier

The practice of law involves a tremendous amount of paper. Even with the advent of the so-called "paperless office," copying documents plays a very large role in the standard law practice. In addition to producing copies of court pleadings for other attorneys, you will need to copy things such as medical records, arrest reports, wills, deeds, letters, and almost any other document moving into or out of your office. Even with many courts using online filing systems and attorneys accepting documents by email, the need for photocopies continues to be strong. And, most of your clients are going to want to receive paper copies from you.

2. Fax

The fax machine is an extremely important communications tool. While many attorneys are still making a minimal use of email and other forms of online communications, the fax machine is almost universally used. You will find that many clients now have their own fax machines at home too. No matter how automated or high tech your office may be, you will need a fax machine.

71

An exception to the need for a fax machine does exist, for those who are tightening their budget or are focusing on a remote or virtual office. Many are now using the services of companies who enable the user to send and receive faxes through email. The fax is converted into a PDF document, which can be viewed on the computer or printed out on paper. Of course, the ability to access faxes this way depends on your computer being operational. If you choose this option, keep in mind that if your computer crashes or your internet service is down, you will also temporarily lose the ability to send and receive faxes. Also, this method will not work for sending documents which are not saved as a file on your computer.

3. *Printer*

There are several different kinds of printers on the market, using various kinds of inks and different methods of printing. You should research the printers on the market to decide which will most interest you. The primary issues are deciding from color, photo, or black and white, and whether to purchase an ink jet or laser printer. The primary disadvantage to color and photo printers, particularly the ink jet versions, is that they consume ink very quickly and tend to be expensive to maintain. A good black and white laser printer can run for a very long time on one toner cartridge. If you do not anticipate a significant amount of color printing being necessary in your practice, it is usually best to be economical and choose a standard black ink laser printer.

4. Computer

You do not need a computer that can play all of your favorite video games with the best graphics and sound. All you need is a good word processing computer that has enough RAM to handle the programs you may need to run for your practice. Do not spend a lot of money on a top-of-the-line computer when you are not going to need it, at least not at this stage of your practice. Just make sure that the computer can handle any law practice management software you need to run, and save the upgrades for later.

5. Typewriter

While seemingly obsolete, the need for the use of a typewriter still arises from time to time. Keep an inexpensive one on hand if you can find one at a low price. It is not essential to starting your practice, but it can be very convenient to have one around.

6. Calculator

You will often need to make basic calculations for various matters, whether in the office or perhaps in the hallway outside the courtroom. Keeping a small calculator handy can be a real lifesaver at times you would not expect to need it.

7. Telephones

There are amazing telephone systems on the market; many of them also come at an amazingly high price. A standard phone system will be sufficient until you start expanding your practice, and can offer many of the same benefits of the expensive system without charging the expensive price. When you get to the stage of hiring a secretary, you will need to look at multi-line phones, intercom systems, etc. For now, get a simple phone that is easy to use, and explore more advanced options later.

For those exploring a virtual office or remote office, there are now phone systems specifically designed for that kind of operation. Your secretary can answer the phone in your office, and then connect the person to your phone even if you are on the other side of the country. To the client, it appears no different than when your secretary transfers the call to your office across the hall.

Office Supplies

The following is a non-exhaustive list of basic office supplies that you will need for starting your practice. These can all be obtained at standard office supply stores for reasonable prices.

1. Copy/printer paper.

2. Manilla file folders.

3. File labels

4. Writing pads.

5. Telephone message books.

6. Pens.

7. Highlighters

8. Sticky notes.

9. Stationery (see discussion in Chapter 7).

10. Postage.

11. Stapler and staples.

12. Paper clips (various sizes).

13. Letter opener.

14. In-box and Out-box.

15. Scissors

16. Tape

17. Receipt books.

CHAPTER SEVEN

Selecting Stationary

The decision over the design for your office letterhead, envelopes, and business cards is probably not the first thing that comes to mind when thinking of opening an office. However, these items will convey an image to clients and prospective clients, as well as to other attorneys dealing with you. The appearance you create with these simple items is far more important than you may expect.

While some attorneys try unconventional styles, or perhaps even include a photograph in the design (similar to the standard practice of real estate agents), it is best to design a somewhat traditional card or letterhead that portrays an image of strength and stability. This may not seem as exciting as the great artistic picture you just designed on your computer, but clients tend to have more confidence in stable and mature attorneys than they have in attorneys trying to be trendy or funny.

With the high quality printing that is now available from laser printers and the availability of high quality paper in office supply stores, an attorney can easily create and print his own letterhead in the office. However, if you still wish to have the traditional embossed or raised letterhead, the easiest approach is to use a business printing shop. All of my letterhead and business cards are printed through a local company that does high-quality work. Whenever my supplies start to run low, my secretary simply calls them to restock our supplies. Since they already have everything set up for our design, it takes very little time for them to provide us with whatever we need printed.

Purchasing quality letterhead and business cards is a smart investment. If your business cards look like you printed them yourself on your own computer and printer, some people may wonder about the quality of your legal services. However, a professional design conveys the image of success you want to create in the minds of prospects. In this business, your image is extremely important, and the business cards that you hand to prospective clients are an extension of that image.

In selecting a design for business cards and letterhead, think carefully about the image you wish to portray. If you have a specialty practice, it is a good idea to indicate this on your business cards. While some recommend having a different card for each area of law that you practice, this seems like a confusing way to try to get people to believe you specialize in their exact needs. If you are practicing in more than one area of law, it would be best to leave off any indication of specialization from the card.

A local printing shop will have a number of designs on hand for you to consider, and most will be willing to create several custom designs for you to compare side-by-side. There are certain ethical regulations that apply to your letterhead and business cards, so review your state's Rules of Professional Conduct before giving final approval to any printer.

CHAPTER EIGHT

Setting And Collecting Fees

The practice of law is a professional service, but it is also a business. As much as you may wish to aid the poor and the oppressed without charging them a fee, the reality is that unless you are independently wealthy you must charge for your services.

Early in my practice, an attorney told me that if he had a choice between working all day for a client and not getting paid, or sitting on his porch all day and not getting paid, he would choose to go home and sit on his porch. The longer I practice law, the more I agree with him. Most of your clients would agree that they would not go to their jobs if their employers were not going to pay them. If they would not work for free, why should you?

The starting point in setting a fee is to prepare a business plan outlining your anticipated expenses and your personal financial requirements. Before you can decide what you are going to charge, you need to determine what amounts you have to make and what amounts you want to make. A simple way to do this is as follows:

Determining the Cost of Staying in Business

First, determine your monthly expenses. This should include not only your fixed expenses like rent, insurance, and phone, but also an average of your variable expenses such as office supplies, seminar fees, books, and costs advanced on contingent fee cases. Take this monthly average, and multiply it by twelve (for the twelve months of the year). This will give you the annual cost of running your business. Now, take that number, and divide it by fifty (working from an estimate that your office will be open fifty weeks of the year instead of fifty-two). This number will tell you the amount you need to earn every week to keep the office open. Divide that number again by five, and you know exactly how much you need to earn every workday to operate your business. Divide again by eight, and you have the cost per hour of operating your business.

As an example, assume for the sake of discussion that it will cost approximately $2,000 per month to operate your practice.[6] Multiply this figure by twelve months, and you see that it will cost you $24,000 per year in business expenses. Divide this sum by fifty (assuming the office is closed the other two weeks of the year), and you will find that you must make $480 per week just to pay the office overhead expenses. Divide that number by five, and you see that you must make $96 per day. If you can bill eight hours per day, this calculation shows that to break even, without earning any personal income, you only need to bring in $12 per hour to meet the expenses chosen for this example.

---

[6] This figure was randomly selected as an example only, and is not suggested as your actual operating expense.

Determining your Personal Income Requirements

Next, think about how much you want, or need, to earn in a year. I would recommend running these figures with different income amounts, ranging from the absolute minimum you have to earn to the amount which would be your dream income.

By way of example, assume that you want to earn $10,000 per month in personal income from your practice, for an annual income of $120,000 per year. Divide this by fifty, and you find that you must earn $2400 per week above expenses to meet your target income. Divide this by five, and you see that you need $480 per day above expenses. Divide again by eight, and you see that you should make $60 per hour above your hourly expense to reach your target income goal.

Determining the Minimum Hourly Income Requirement

Now, armed with your hourly expenses and your hourly personal income goal, it is quite simple to determine what you must earn per hour to meet your goals. In our example, an hourly cost of $12 per hour combines with your personal $60 per hour to give you a minimum fee of $72 per hour. Thus, the attorney in this example must set a goal of earning an average of around $75 per hour to meet his or her overall income goals.

Unfortunately, this does not necessarily mean that you will actually earn $75 per hour (or whatever number you have chosen) for your time at work, especially in the early days when you are first building your practice. For example, if you only have an average of 20 hours per week of billable time, you would have to be earning $150 per hour to hit the target income in the example.

Another issue relates to your need to expand your practice. Your bills may be low at first if you do not start out with a secretary, but eventually you will want to add at least one employee. Have you chosen an hourly fee that will allow you to add employees when enough of your hours are filled with work? It is best to establish your fees based on the expectation that your expenses will increase.

Calculations using this formula are useful for setting income goals, and are also useful in determining your hourly fee rate. However, remember that you are likely to have certain matters you are handling on a contingency fee basis, and others for which you have charged a flat fee. It is a little more difficult to attach an hourly value to these kinds of cases, but as a general rule make sure that the fee you will receive on cases of that nature equals or exceeds what you would have reasonably expected to earn if the work was performed at an hourly charge.

Ethical Issues in Setting Fees

The free market does not freely apply in dealing with the practice of law, and there is more to setting a fee than simply deciding how much you want to put in your pocket. While most parties outside of our profession are free to enter into contracts which contain any lawful terms upon which they both can agree, attorneys are faced with oversight and limitations from the bar association. There are certain fee arrangements that may be legal, but to the bar association are unethical, excessive, or at least inappropriate.

Under each state's rules of professional responsibility, there are a number of factors for the attorney to consider in establishing his or her fee for a particular case. While the rules provide the relevant factors to consider in setting a fee, they do not provide any means by which one can make a mathematical calculation. Rather, the states impose regulations which prohibit unreasonable fees and expenses, and take into account factors such as the time constraints and difficulties of the case, the fees typically charged in the community for similar services, the experience and reputation of the lawyer, and whether the fee is fixed or contingent.

Ultimately, the issue of whether or not the fee is unreasonable is a matter of opinion (the opinion of your state bar, that is) more than it is a matter of mathematics. As a starting point, consider your comfort level in charging the fee. As a new attorney, you will be uncomfortable quoting any fee on a case, so do not let generic hesitancy and nervousness make the determination. However, the reasonableness of a fee is often a matter of common sense. Attorneys do not get in trouble for fee decisions upon which reasonable people may disagree. Sanctions on unreasonable fees are generally reserved for those attorneys who have exploited their clients by acting in a manner which is obviously unreasonable and inappropriate.

In addition to the ethical issues regarding the reasonableness of a fee, the bar associations have set restrictions on the fee arrangements which can be made in certain types of cases. These are discussed below under sections dealing with specific kinds of fees. Each state bar association may have additional restrictions on the type of fee which may be charged. For example, state bar associations will not tolerate an attorney exchanging legal services for sexual favors from a client. Most states also prohibit accepting criminal cases on a contingent fee basis. Review the rules of professional conduct which apply to lawyers in your state to determine the details on charging an ethical fee.

Types of Fees

There are a number of fee structures which attorneys may use for charging clients for their services. The standard fee structure is to charge a flat fee, hourly fee, or contingent fee. However, several variations and hybrids have emerged as options for attorneys as well. Several fee structures are described below. Sample fee contracts for certain fee agreements are contained in Chapter Twelve of this book.

1. Flat fee

Attorneys charge flat fees in cases where they are billing by the service performed, rather than by the hour. For example, it is common for lawyers to charge a flat fee (in advance) for most criminal offenses. Likewise, services for drafting deeds, wills, or uncontested divorces are commonly charged as a flat fee. Flat fee cases are typically those that the attorney handles on a routine basis where he or she can easily estimate the amount of time and effort the case will require. However, it is always wise to advise the client that the flat fee is for the attorney's fees only, and that any expenses will have to be paid by the client. Otherwise, you could unexpectedly be hit with expenses that consume most of the fee you collected, or even exceed it.

Flat fees provide the client the benefit of knowing exactly what the entire fee will be for the service provided. Sometimes the attorney comes out ahead on a flat fee arrangement if the services can be performed more quickly or easily than expected, and other times the attorney can severely underestimate the work he or she will have to perform to earn the fee. The ability to estimate an appropriate flat fee is a skill that you will acquire and develop as you gain more and more experience in your practice.

In setting a flat fee on a case, an attorney should balance the ethical factors required by the state bar association, and try to get a general idea of the fees commonly charged in the community for that kind of representation. Attorneys generally do not mind telling you what they charge on certain routine cases that come along on a regular basis, and you will find a broad range of fees in your market. In my practice, I no longer consider the fees charged by other attorneys for similar services, because I know what my services are worth and how much time it will take to provide quality services to my clients. However, when I first started my practice, I sought the advice of other attorneys simply because I had no idea of where to begin in setting fees. Once you have a basic idea of standard fees, you will quickly learn which situations require an increased fee and which ones can be handled at a lower price.

The standard procedure is to request the flat fee in advance, but often an attorney will agree to a payment plan for clients who cannot afford the entire fee in advance. In agreeing to a payment plan, the best practice is to make sure that the payments are high enough that you will receive your entire fee prior to the end of the representation of the client. Your chances of getting paid the full fee are greatly reduced once the case is over. The motivation to pay the lawyer is much higher when there is an upcoming court date than there is once the matter is finally resolved.

If you choose to accept a payment plan on a flat fee, make sure that you require some kind of down payment from the client before commencing any work. Remember, if the client is unable or unwilling to invest his or her own funds in getting the case started, they are unlikely to be cooperative in paying the remaining attorney's fees later. The best practice is to get a down payment of 50% of the fee in advance, but allow yourself some flexibility on the issue. The key is to get a down payment that is high enough to demonstrate that the client is serious about the case, and to make it worth your time to be in the case even if you have trouble collecting the rest of the fee.[7]

---

[7] If you are dealing with a jurisdiction where you cannot withdraw from a case once you have entered an appearance, as a general rule you should not accept a payment plan arrangement. You do not want to get stuck in a case where you cannot withdraw for nonpayment.

If you are going to let your clients finance their fee payments with you, try to make an accurate determination of a reasonable amount that the client can pay each week or month. I have learned that it is much better to have a client who faithfully makes a smaller payment every week than it is to have a client who promises large payments but delivers inconsistently or not at all. However, when considering how lenient to be with a client on payment arrangements, keep in mind that many people could call a relative and borrow the fee instead of relying on your generosity. Whenever possible, let a client's family members be the ones who finance the the case, not you. I have had numerous experiences where I refused to accept a payment plan from a client who claimed poverty, and then received my full fee within a day or two from a family member of a client.

While the best method of practice is to have the client sign a fee contract, most states do not require written contracts in flat fee cases. Review your state bar regulations to determine when you must use a contract and when it is optional.

A dispute over a flat fee is not likely to arise unless the attorney seeks to withdraw before completion of the representation, or unless the client believed that the attorney would be providing more or better services than the attorney delivered or was willing to do. Regardless of whether or not it is mandatory in your state, the best way to avoid disputes in the future is to put the agreement in writing at the commencement of the representation. It does not take that much additional time to fill out your form contract and obtain the client's signature. At a minimum, send the client a letter outlining the services which will be provided for the fee. The case where you do not take this precaution may later be the case where you regret it.

2. *Hourly Fee*

When a case is handled on an hourly fee basis, the client is charged specifically for the time actually spent by the attorney on the case. Some firms also bill for paralegal and secretarial time at a reduced rate, and others simply absorb those costs as being included in the attorney's hourly fee. The standard practice in an hourly fee case is for the attorney to obtain a retainer from the client in advance of actually performing work on the case. This retainer should be sufficient to cover what the attorney expects to bill in attorney's fees during the initial month of representation. Once that retainer is exhausted, the client is expected to post an additional retainer.

The purpose of the retainer is clear and simple: to make sure the attorney gets paid. If the client does not have the funds to pay you a retainer today, there is no reason to believe the client can pay it next month when he or she receives your first bill. Requiring a retainer up front also forces the client to make an investment in his or her own case. If the client does not have enough belief or interest in the case to post a retainer to pay for your time, then the client is not likely to pay for your services or provide much in the way of assistance in the pursuit of the case. If you choose to accept an hourly fee case with no money paid in advance, assume that you will not get paid.

An exception to this rule may exist in dealing with certain large companies or with certain clients with whom you have an ongoing or repeated attorney-client relationship. Certain companies expect to be billed monthly for the work you have performed, and will write you a check shortly after receiving your bill. If you are having trouble collecting your fees from such a company, advise them that they must pay their bills promptly or start posting a retainer in advance. Remember that there are some companies which attempt to avoid or delay payment of their bills as long as possible. While some attorneys are nervous about insulting or irritating a client, you do not lose anything by losing a client who does not pay your bill.

What should you charge as your hourly rate? To make this determination, you need to go back to the calculations you made at the start of this chapter. Your time is valuable, and your income is based on how you spend your time. Every hour you spend working for one client is an hour that you did not work for someone else. Every hour that you work for a non-paying client reduces your income by whatever amount you needed to earn that hour. And every hour you work for a paying client puts more money in your pocket and gets you closer to meeting your income goals. Determine your costs, your personal needs, and your desired income, and set your fees appropriately.

In order to bill a client on an hourly basis, you must maintain time sheets documenting your work and the time expended on it. You should also bill the client promptly for that work every month. It is generally wise to give a detailed description of each item on the client's bill, to make sure the client understands how you are earning your fee.

3. Contingent Fees

Contingent fees are best known for their use in personal injury cases, particularly automobile accidents. In such a case, the attorney does not charge the client a fee in advance, nor does the attorney charge an hourly fee. Instead, the attorney agrees to work on the case on the condition that he or she receives a percentage of the amount of money ultimately recovered on behalf of the client. In automobile accident cases, the standard percentage in most places is 33%. Products liability cases are often handled on a 40% contingent fee, and medical malpractice claims commonly require a 50% contingent fee. Debt collections cases are sometimes charged on a contingent fee basis of anywhere between 25% to 50%. In addition to the contingent fee, the attorney receives reimbursement for all costs advanced to pursue the client's case. That reimbursement comes out of the client's percentage of the recovery.

Contingent fee cases have the potential to generate the largest fees for attorneys, but they also create the risk of getting nothing. Thus, contingent fee cases must be carefully screened for merit. They also require a significant amount of the attorney's time without any compensation at the time of performing the work. Some contingent fee cases, such as products liability lawsuits, can require years to reach a resolution, so the attorney has to be prepared to survive off of other cases during that time. This is one of the reasons that many attorneys simply refer these cases to specialty firms.

A common practice in personal injury cases is for attorneys to make referrals to attorneys or firms who specialize in the specific type of case involved. In exchange for the referral, the new firm will pay the referring attorney a percentage of the recovery as a referral fee. In most places, the standard referral fee is 33%. This referral fee comes out of the attorney's fees, not out of the client's portion of the fee. Thus, the client pays nothing extra as a result of the referral.

Referral fees are subject to regulation by your state bar association, and may have particular restrictions or complications in your state. Make sure you review your state's particular version of this rule, as many states have added or modified the requirements of this rule. In fact, most states prohibit contingent fees in domestic relations or criminal cases.

For the most part, contingent fee arrangements should be reserved for claims where you are fairly certain that you will receive a considerable recovery on behalf of the client. Otherwise, the fee you ultimately earn on the case may be substantially below your standard hourly income. Some attorneys have an average income of $1000 per hour or more based on their contingent fee work, but they do not achieve that rate by taking bad cases. Only accept a contingent fee where your case is strong and the amount of recovery will generate a fee significantly higher than your standard hourly target income.

4. Combination Fees

In some cases, attorneys choose to enter into a fee agreement with a client involving a combination of the standard (hourly, flat, or contingent) fee structures. For example, an attorney may agree to handle certain cases at a reduced hourly rate but also receive a contingent fee of some percentage at the end. The same may be done through a combination of a flat fee up front, and a contingent fee at the conclusion of the case. In other situations, an attorney may say that certain stages of a case can be handled for a flat fee or series of fees, but that beyond a certain point the case will be billed on an hourly fee basis. Whether to enter into a hybrid fee arrangement is a decision to be made in the particular circumstances of the case.

Lawsuits to Collect Attorney's Fees

Some attorneys file lawsuits against people they have represented to recover unpaid attorneys fees. The frustration from not being paid for your efforts is understandable, and typically the clients who should appreciate your efforts the most are the ones least likely to pay. Nonetheless, it is generally a bad idea to sue a client for not paying the bill. When you sue a client, you are often going to draw a retaliation from the client in the form of a bar complaint alleging that you charged an excessive fee or somehow screwed up his or her case. At a minimum, they will likely defend their nonpayment by alleging that you did not provide the full services that were agreed upon, or that you charged an unreasonable fee. While you will usually prevail in this kind of bar complaint or lawsuit, most attorneys do not consider it to be worth the time and hassle they will have to go through to collect the fee. Further, it is generally a bad idea to develop a reputation of being the attorney that sues his or her own clients. When you do not get paid, the best solution is for you to accept the nonpayment as a learning experience at your own expense, and remember it the next time someone does not want to pay for your services in advance.

CHAPTER NINE

Hiring A Secretary

Hiring a good secretary is one of the best investments an attorney can ever make. The big question is not if you will hire a secretary, but when. Even if you are running a "virtual office," it is very likely that at some point you will want to hire an assistant to help you maintain efficiency and increase your productivity.

When do you need a secretary

A new attorney does not need a secretary, because he or she does not have any clients in the first place. It usually takes a few months to get to the point where a secretary changes from a luxury item to a necessity.

I decided to hire my first secretary when my practice reached the point that I did not have time to do my own secretarial work any longer, and I was working day and night to get everything done by myself. When I hired a secretary, there was someone to open files, make photocopies, send letters, draw up uncontested divorce packages, plug information into my will forms, and many other tasks that I was doing by myself up to that point. Suddenly, I found myself with more free time, as well as more time that I could put towards performing actual legal work on my cases.

A good rule of thumb is that the time to hire a secretary is when it is costing you more to be without one than it would cost to have one. Always remember that your time has a value - whether you are billing clients for it, or just trying to spend time enjoying your own life. Think of how much time you are spending practicing law, and compare it to how much time you are spending on administrative tasks (such as opening files, billing, photocopying, filing, going to the post office for stamps, etc.) that are not billable to your clients. If you are doing it all by yourself within a forty-hour week, then you probably don't need a secretary. But if you are doing legal work all day, and then spending your evenings doing secretarial tasks, then you are at the point where it becomes sensible to hire an assistant. Even if you just start someone on a part-time basis, it can make a huge transformation in your practice. Most attorneys who hire a part-time secretary move them to full-time shortly thereafter.

How to choose a secretary

Choosing to hire a secretary is much easier than selecting which secretary to hire. There are many competing issues to consider. Some attorneys want to hire experienced secretaries, because they already know how to do their job and can be more efficient and useful sooner. Other attorneys prefer to get younger and less experienced secretaries. They do this not only because it is less expensive, but because the attorney wants to train the secretary in his or her own way of handling cases.

For the new attorney, if money is not a problem, then it may be wise to hire an experienced secretary. Many new lawyers will be surprised to learn how little they actually know about practicing law, and will find an experienced legal secretary to be valuable in getting to know the local procedures. How many new attorneys know, or possess, all of the forms necessary to obtain a simple uncontested divorce? While law school teaches the basics of handling a case, there are standard procedures, forms, and methods of processing documents through the courthouse that you will not know until you have gone through the process. An experienced secretary will already know how to handle these steps.

Most new attorneys are afraid of incurring the expense of hiring a secretary, and this is a reasonable fear if you are overextending yourself financially. However, there is a saying that "a good secretary doesn't cost you money, she makes you money." You will be surprised how much your income and efficiency will improve if you have the right person working for you.

Where to find a secretary

Where do you find a secretary? Many lawyers will put up notices at local colleges that have paralegal or legal secretary programs. Some will ask their friends, associates, and other attorneys for recommendations. Often other attorneys can direct you to someone who has worked as a legal secretary, or perhaps worked as a clerk at the courthouse. Some may contact an employment agency to send referrals. But the way that will lead to the largest number of resumes landing on your desk is to simply run a notice in the classified ads of your local newspaper. Every person looking for a job as a legal secretary will get their resume to you.

I particularly like the approach of receiving resumes through the mail, because most applicants will draft a cover letter to go with their resume. One of the best ways to measure the quality of the work this person would do for you is to evaluate his or her cover letter. If this person is well-spoken and professional on paper, then it is likely that this person could do a good job writing letters and documents for you. If, however, the letter contains bad grammar, spelling errors, or other obvious mistakes, then that should raise red flags for you. While you should remember that the job applicant is not likely to have your level of education, and therefore may not be as proficient a writer as you, a person with poor grammar skills will have problems assisting you with this kind of work.

How to decide who to hire

What should you look for in a secretary? Apart from the obvious balancing of experience versus price, the decision over who to hire boils down to a few key factors. While it is hard to know whether a candidate possesses these traits, you should do your best to ascertain whether this person has certain qualities that will make him or her a good employee.

First, does this person seem to be honest? The last thing you need in your office is someone who cannot be trusted. There are numerous horror stories about secretaries who pocketed fees from clients, and even those who took money from the attorney's trust account for personal use.[8] There are many things you can do to help protect yourself from such risks, but the best starting point is to hire someone who seems to have integrity.

Is this someone who will be dependable? I have had secretaries with many different backgrounds and situations, and it appears that the individual's character has more to do with dependability than any other factor. People with similar life situations will handle their personal responsibilities differently. Ultimately, a person's work ethic, not their circumstances, will determine the quality and dependability of the services provided to you.

Do you believe this person will be loyal? There are some people who, despite how good you may treat them, are going to talk badly about you behind your back. Or, they may simply be the type who constantly hunt for a better job. As an attorney, you are not looking to hire someone on a short-term basis. You do not want to invest time and energy training someone as a secretary, only for them to leave you for another job while you have to start over with someone new.

Does this person have a stable employment history? One of the important points to consider in evaluating a resume is that person's employment history. I would be inclined to hire someone who was less qualified but who had a stable employment history before I would hire the more qualified person who seems to jump from job to job every six months to a year. I have seen resumes from

---

[8] NEVER put your secretary on your bank accounts, especially not your trust account. This rule applies even if your secretary is your spouse. There have been too many attorneys over the years who have lost their licenses over financial mismanagement that was actually committed by a trusted assistant.

applicants who listed an impressive array of past employers. The only problem was that the person did not stay with any of them for very long. The stable person is more likely to be with you on a long-term basis, while the other may leave you looking for a new secretary next year.

Does this person have a good personality? Is this someone who has a good "phone voice," someone who will put potential clients in a good mood when they walk in the door, and someone you enjoy talking to? Remember that this person will usually have contact with your clients more often than you do. Thus, to a large extent, this person will create the image of your firm. Also consider the fact that you will be spending every day with this person - all day, every day of the workweek. At times, you will be around your secretary more than you are around your spouse. Will the person you are considering get on your nerves over time, or will this person make your work a more enjoyable experience?

Much of the final decision will be made on instinct. After weighing the pros and cons of each, you will be able to narrow down the list to a few candidates, but at some point there are only a few differentiating points to consider. When two or more similarly qualified applicants are asking for the job, your instincts will help you make the right choice. And if it turns out to be the wrong choice, simply consider it as a learning experience, and do a better job in hiring the next one. You will always learn more from your mistakes than from the things you do correctly.

CHAPTER TEN

Marketing Your Practice

Marketing is a broad term encompassing the many different ways to promote your practice. You are choosing the message about yourself that you want to send to the public. The ultimate goal is to bring in paying clients who can enable you to build a successful career. The key is to determine what kind of clients you want to reach, and then tailor your message to reach them.

Defining Your Image

The first step in planning to market your practice is to decide what image you want to project to the public. Part of this decision will be made based on what areas of practice you have selected as your preferred specializations. Part will be based on what you want people to think when they think of you. Remember, if you want people to choose you as their attorney, you should be ready to tell them why. Your image and message should be targeted to the kinds of clients you want to represent.

General Ethics in Advertising

Before starting to advertise or market your services, review the rules of your state bar association. While most attorneys know the basic rules such as the prohibition on paying referral fees to non-lawyers, or the requirement of disclaimers on ads, there are many nuances to the rules that you may not have previously considered. Also, your state bar association may have issued ethics opinions regarding certain kinds of advertising, and you should make sure you have reviewed these as well. For example, some states prohibit attorneys from buying ad space on pharmacy prescription bags or from including their firm brochure in the local "Welcome Wagon" gift bags.

Business Cards & Letterhead

This subject is addressed in more detail in Chapter Seven. However, it merits mentioning here that your business cards and stationary are going to be the form of written communication people see most often coming out of your office. If your letterhead appears sloppy and unprofessional, people may assume that you are a sloppy and unprofessional lawyer. Likewise, the use of professional letterhead projects an image of competence and reliability.

If you are putting out any effort at networking, you will go through business cards very quickly. When you are introduced to people, the natural step should be to hand them your business card. With a little practice, you can make this appear as a casual and friendly act, rather than a brazen attempt to recruit business. You want that future client to be favorably impressed with you, and that impression includes the professionalism of the card you are holding out in your hand. Every minute you spend struggling to find the perfect design for your cards and letterhead (which should coordinate with each other) will be well worth the effort over the years to come.

Networking

It is no exaggeration to say that "word of mouth" is the best form of advertising. Referrals will lead to having more quality clients than any other form of marketing. Meeting people and telling them what you do is the essence of networking. Your goal in networking is to make people remember you, so that when they need an attorney or are asked to recommend an attorney, they will think of you.

One thing to keep in mind is that you should give people a positive reason to remember you. If someone remembers you as the attorney who got drunk and made a fool of himself at the Chamber of Commerce banquet, they are not likely to hire you and they will discourage others from hiring you too. But if you were the attorney who was friendly, well-spoken, and confident, then you will come to mind when they need legal representation.

1. Community Service

A popular way to network with potential clients is to join a community service organization. This will place you side-by-side with people who are volunteering their time to help with a cause that is important to them, and your involvement will make a positive impression on people while improving your community at the same time. If you choose to become involved in community organizations, make sure to choose positions or issues you truthfully support. Do not pretend to be someone you are not.

Connections and friendships made through volunteer work have a long-lasting nature, and your involvement in one project today could lead to referrals coming in to you ten or more years from now. For example, a person I had not seen in many years referred his girlfriend to me recently when she was in a car accident and needed an attorney. Even though he and I had not maintained contact over the years, other than occasionally running into each other around town, when he needed an attorney he thought of me because I was the one he knew personally. My involvement in various civic organizations has been a tremendous boost to my practice, as it has given me an opportunity to get to know potential clients on a personal basis instead of just being a name in the phone book.

2. *Religious Organizations*

Attending church, temple, or other services within your particular religious affiliation is a great way to meet clients. While client recruitment should not be your reason for getting involved in your local church, it is certainly a benefit that comes from it. In a church setting, it is wise to be less aggressive in handing out business cards than you may be at your Kiwanis Club meeting. You would not want to create the impression you are in church looking for business. Allow the issue of "what do you do" to come up naturally in the conversation, and pass on the card in a friendly manner of simply letting the person how to get in touch with you if your assistance is ever needed.

3. *Networking Clubs*

The importance of networking is so recognized that various clubs and organizations have formed whose purpose is to introduce business professionals to each other. The concept is to provide an opportunity for people to meet each other, talk about their businesses, pass out business cards, and secure clients/customers and referrals. This is a very direct and efficient way to network in your community, and is good practice for developing your skills at meeting potential clients.

4. Friends and Family

Friends and family are an important source of business and referrals. It is important that you let them know that you have started your own practice, and that you are accepting new clients. Make sure they have your business cards, so it is easy for them to remember how to contact you when they or their friends need an attorney. Make sure to communicate to them that if they or their friends have a legal need, even if it is in an area you do not handle, they should come to you so you can refer them to the best attorney for their particular problem. The important thing is to get the people coming in the door.

5. Clients

Never forget the importance of making your clients happy. At some point, your client will be asked by someone if he or she knows a good attorney. Do you want them to say, "Oh, call this attorney, he handled a problem for me and did a great job?" Or, do you want them to say, "Well, whatever you do, don't call the guy I hired. He was a jerk."

There is no better way to get a client than a referral from an existing client. There is also no better way to lose a potential client than by one of your clients trashing your reputation. In this line of work, you will never make everyone happy, and there will be clients who think you should have done a better job. But if the majority of your clients feel that you did a good job for them, or that you put out a strong effort for them even if you did not succeed, then your business will grow stronger and stronger over time.

Many attorneys take the additional step of writing to clients and encouraging them to make referrals. I have always felt that if your client is satisfied with the services you are providing, then they will make the referrals without a letter from you pushing them to send you business. While such letters could lead to more referrals, they could also create the impression that your business is struggling and that you are having trouble getting clients, so be careful as to your choice of words. You should also make sure that any request for referrals does not violate your state bar's ethical rules. Mentioning referrals in a letter at the conclusion of a client's case is certainly appropriate, but sending letters to your clients specifically pushing for referrals will not create a very good image of your firm.

Internet

Building a strong presence on the internet is very important in building your practice. It is absolutely essential that you have a professional website about yourself and your practice. It should be a website where you own the name as well, rather than a back page off of a mass market internet directory.

Many companies will try to charge you to be listed in their attorney search engines. However, there are many sites on the web who will list your practice for free if you simply fill out an online form. Your real goal in internet marketing and in being listed on free legal directories is to drive clients to your website. Once they get to your website, you want them to be impressed with what they see and choose to contact you about their problem.

If a person is looking for an attorney on the internet, it is very likely he or she will also do online research about that attorney. Thus, your website should project a strong professional image. It is also helpful if you name appears in news articles from time to time, because these will appear online as well and create the appearance that you are a prominent attorney. Anything that makes you appear to be important in the community - whether for your law practice, your civic involvements, whatever - can help with convincing potential clients to select you as their attorney.

Announcements

Some books on the subject of starting a law practice advise attorneys to mail out formal engraved announcements to everyone on every conceivable mailing list they can acquire. While this may be a good idea in theory, there are some problems with this idea in practice. Blanketing your state with fancy announcement cards may be good for your self-image, but it does not accomplish much beyond depleting the funds you need for opening your office. If you have a large operating budget, then feel free to send announcements to as many people as you want. However, if you are working on a tight budget, you should be very conservative about how many people received an engraved announcement from you. The printing costs for this kind of announcement are rather high, and the postage to mail out hundreds of these cards will add up quickly. For the most part, if the recipient of your announcement does not know you, the announcement is in front of the reader just for the length of time it takes to remove it from the envelope and throw it in the trash.

Even the people who know you are not likely to save a formal notice that you have opened a law practice, unless it is your grandmother or someone who would have an interest in collecting things about your life. However, a business card enclosed with a letter is very likely to land in someone's wallet or on their refrigerator door. A classy business card that is kept in a Rolodex is a much better investment than a classy announcement that goes into the trash.

Yellow Pages

Placing an advertisement in your local yellow pages is a great form of advertising, as long as you can afford it. I have always maintained a full page advertisement in my local phone company's yellow pages directory, and it was one of the best investments I have made in my practice. The first month my full page ad appeared in the yellow pages, I immediately saw a huge increase in the number of calls I received. While the ad was expensive, it easily paid for itself every month. However, I had the advantage of starting my practice in a small town, where the advertising rates were significantly lower than those in the bigger cities. If you are starting in a big city where yellow pages advertising may cost thousands of dollars per month, you will probably have to start with a smaller ad when you first enter the phone book.

At one time, the only "yellow pages" a person would be reviewing would be the version published by the local phone company. These days, there are multiple phone books in each community. While these can also be valuable sources of business, be careful not to get drawn into advertising in too many of these publications. There is a point of diminishing returns, at which it starts costing you more to run all of those ads than you are generating in business from them. Choose the one phone book that you expect most people will use - typically the one published by the local phone company - and focus your investment there.

If you are unable to afford a big ad, it is still a good idea to try to get a small one placed in the book, even if it is merely a small box in the directory listing. Someone is still more likely to call the number in the small advertisement than they are to scan through all of the attorney names in the general directory and stop on your name. Check into the rates available in your area, and see if yellow pages advertising is for you.

Local Publications

Advertisements in local newspapers and community newsletters can be a good way to market your practice to a niche market. While generic newspaper ads are not overly effective, they can be useful. When first starting your practice, you should consider placing an ad in local newspapers announcing that you are now accepting new clients in the community. This will lead people in need of basic legal matters, such as wills, deeds, etc., to consider coming to you. While you are not likely to land a major murder trial off of an announcement of the opening of your practice, you are likely to get hired to take care of simple matters that people need handled.

Television

"Have you been injured in a car accident?" Anyone who has watched television late at night or in the middle of the day is familiar with attorney television advertising. These ads are targeted towards a very precise market - people who have been injured in an accident and are sitting at home trying to recover, or are awake late at night because they are in too much pain to sleep. This is the perfect example of targeting your advertisement to the audience you want to reach.

Many attorneys are surprised to discover that advertising on local television channels is surprisingly economical. Ads across a spectrum of channels can usually be purchased through a local cable advertising company for a reasonable package price. The key with television advertising is to create the right ad and to run it consistently. You need to consider your target audience, and make a quality commercial that will appeal to that specific group. A television commercial advertising a general practice is not going to bring as good a return as a commercial advertising for a specific area of work. Also, certain areas of practice are not going to generate enough income to justify the expense of filming a commercial and running it on local stations. Television commercials should be targeted towards a niche market in order to have the most effect.

If you are going to run commercials, make sure that they are a good quality production. Do not let Uncle Henry film you with his camcorder. Remember that your commercial will be going into the homes of your potential clients, and they will form an image of you based on that ad. If you are a trial lawyer, you are also projecting an image of yourself to the people who may be sitting on the jury of your next case. If you are going to be one of the lawyers on television, make sure that you are remembered as the one who appears professional and sincere.

Managing Phone Calls From Potential Clients

Books on building a law practice tell you to return all of the phone calls that come into your office. Yet attorneys are notorious for not returning phone calls. The problem for most attorneys with large practices is simply a lack of time. There are only so many phone calls you can take in a day, especially when you are meeting with clients and/or running to court. As a result, the attorneys with larger practices tend to be more selective about which calls they actually return.

However, this book is about *starting* a law practice, and if you are reading this book it is because you are trying to build up your initial clientele. As a new attorney, you do not have the luxury of picking and choosing which calls are the most important to return, and you do not have the excuse of a lack of time because you do not have that much to do. Make sure that you return all of those phone calls unless it is absolutely impossible. When you have built up your practice you can be more careless about ignoring potential business if you choose to take that risk. For now, if someone calls you about being their lawyer, you need to call them back as soon as you can. Remember, a potential client will only wait so long before calling another lawyer.

Some people call one law office after another trying to get a lawyer on the phone. I cannot recall the number of times I have been retained by a client simply because I was the attorney who returned the call. This was particularly true in the early stages of my practice, when I had plenty of time to talk to people. When you are the one returning the call, it creates the impression that you are the attorney who is interested in the case. Likewise, there have been times when I delayed in returning a call, only to discover that the person had already hired another attorney by the time I called. For people who are just picking an attorney out of the phone book, the decision over which attorney to use will be based upon who makes a good connection with them first.

Some people speak to several attorneys before choosing which one to hire. There have been a number of times where I was not the first attorney who returned the call, but I was still the one that was hired to handle the case. How do you make yourself stand out as the best attorney for the job? By simply taking the time to explain to the client the legal issues involved in the case and the options in how to approach it. Taking the time to explain how the system works creates the impression that you are the one who is more knowledgeable about the system - even if you are not.

One precaution in dealing with calls from potential clients is to avoid giving out free legal advice. While you want to convey enough knowledge to create confidence that you are the attorney to hire, you do not want to tell the person so much that they no longer have a need to hire you. The purpose of returning a phone call is to get the person to lock into an appointment in your office, where you can get them to sign a fee contract and write you a check.

Also, remember that while the advice you give out on the phone may be free, you may have professional liability for the consequences of that advice. A person who never actually hired you as an attorney could claim to a court, or at least to your state bar association, that they relied upon your bad advice to their detriment. Whenever someone is trying to get too much information over the phone, just keep emphasizing the need to sit down with them and go over the details in person so that you can give them the most accurate and reliable advice.

Written Communications

A good way to impress your clients is to bury them with paperwork. When you file anything with the court, send your client a copy to review. While your client may not understand a word of what you have sent them, he or she will be glad to see a tangible sign that you are working on the case. It is wise to send your client something in writing at least once a month, even if it is just a reminder notice about their next court date or a letter giving them a status update. Much of a lawyer's work happens outside the presence of the clients, so clients often do not realize just how much (or how little) you actually work on their case. Sending them written documents builds their confidence in your efforts.

Lawyer Referral Services

Many state and local bar associations operate a lawyer referral service. Individuals who need an attorney contact that service and inform them of the general nature of the problem, and the service provides them with a name or list of names of attorneys handling that type of case. Registration on a lawyer referral service is usually optional, and is not automatic. Most services will require proof of professional liability insurance before placing you on their referral list. Some lawyer referral services are advertised, and can be a good source of business for a new attorney. If a client calls the bar association and asks for the name of an attorney to handle a problem, they will assume that your name was given to them because you are a reliable attorney and will almost certainly call you.

Letters to Prospective Clients

Some attorneys make unsolicited direct contact with prospective clients, usually by contacting the individuals by mail. This is particularly common in bankruptcy cases, where attorneys monitor the names of people named as defendants in new lawsuits, and then send a letter to the defendant advising him or her of the right to file bankruptcy. Other attorneys may monitor arrest records to contact those who have new criminal charges, or may follow accident reports to locate potential personal injury clients.

The ethics of such a practice are questionable, and most state bar associations have restrictions on this kind of attorney marketing. Before considering anything of this nature, it would be advisable not only to read your state's rules of professional conduct, but to consult with your state bar association for more details on how you can do this without running afoul of any ethical prohibitions. Or, you could take the approach of most attorneys, and not engage in this type of marketing at all.

CHAPTER ELEVEN

Legal Research

Paying For It

While in law school, you probably had free access to one or more of the major legal research databases. Now that you are out on your own, you will have to pay for legal research out of your own pocket. Before purchasing a subscription to a legal research service, check with your state bar association and professional organizations to which you belong to see if they offer a free service as part of your membership or if they have negotiated a discount rate with any company. For example, several states now provide free access to Casemaker's legal database as part of bar membership.

There are many subscription legal research services available, and their prices vary widely. It is recommended that you review each of them carefully to determine both your research needs and your budget. Some of the better known services include:

Casemaker	www.casemaker.com
Fastcase	www.fastcase.com
LexisNexis	www.lexis.com
LoisLaw	www.loislaw.com
VersusLaw	www.versuslaw.com
Westlaw	www.westlaw.com

Prices range from less than $20 per month to well over $300 per month, depending on which service or which options you select. Be careful not to subscribe to more than you can afford to buy or to which you frequently need access.

Getting It For Free

There are numerous sites on the internet where legal research materials are available without charge. Many of these are operated by state and local governments, some are operated by universities and law schools, and some are maintained by private individuals who pay for the service through links and advertising. These sites can provide legal research, updates on changes in the law, forms, and sometimes practice advice. A simple internet search can lead to many free resources in the relevant jurisdiction. A listing of some of the better resources available are provided on the following pages.

Legal Metasites

Alllaw
www.alllaw.com

Cornell Legal Information Institute
www.law.cornell.edu

Findlaw
www.findlaw.com

Heiros Gamos
www.hg.org

Law Practice Resources
www.lawpracticeresources.com

FEDERAL RESOURCES

United States Constitution
http://www.house.gov/house/Educate.shtml
http://www.usconstitution.net/
http://www.law.cornell.edu/constitution

United States Code
http://thomas.loc.gov/
http://www.gpoaccess.gov/uscode/index.html
http://www.law.cornell.edu/uscode/
http://uscode.house.gov/lawrevisioncounsel.shtml

Code of Federal Regulations
http://www.gpoaccess.gov/cfr/index.html

Congressional Record
http://thomas.loc.gov/

Federal Judicial System
United States Court System
http://www.uscourts.gov/

Administrative Office of the U.S. Courts PACER
Service Center
http://pacer.psc.uscourts.gov/

Federal Courts Finder
http://www.law.emory.edu/FEDCTS/

Federal Rules of Bankruptcy Procedure
http://www.law.cornell.edu/rules/frbp/

Federal Rules of Criminal Procedure
http://www.law.cornell.edu/rules/frcrmp/

Federal Rules of Evidence
http://www.law.cornell.edu/rules/fre/

UNITED STATES SUPREME COURT

http://www.supremecourtus.gov/
http://www.findlaw.com/casecode/supreme.html
http://www.supremecourtus.gov

The Supreme Court Historical Society
http://www.supremecourthistory.org/

U.S. COURTS OF APPEALS

First Circuit Court of Appeals
http://www.ca1.uscourts.gov/
http://www.law.emory.edu/1circuit/

Second Circuit Court of Appeals
http://www.ca2.uscourts.gov/

Third Circuit Court of Appeals
http://www.ca3.uscourts.gov/

Fourth Circuit Court of Appeals
http://www.ca4.uscourts.gov/

Fifth Circuit Court of Appeals
http://www.ca5.uscourts.gov/

Sixth Circuit Court of Appeals
http://www.ca6.uscourts.gov/

Seventh Circuit Court of Appeals
http://www.ca7.uscourts.gov/

Eighth Circuit Court of Appeals
http://www.ca8.uscourts.gov/

Ninth Circuit Court of Appeals
http://www.ca9.uscourts.gov/

Tenth Circuit Court of Appeals
http://www.ck10.uscourts.gov/

Eleventh Circuit Court of Appeals
http://www.ca11.uscourts.gov/

**Court of Appeals for the District of
Columbia Circuit**
http://www.cadc.uscourts.gov/

Court of Appeals for the Federal Circuit
http://www.fedcir.gov/

INTERNATIONAL LAW

Heiros Gamos
http://www.hg.org/

United States Department of State
http://state.gov/

United Nations
http://un.org/

European Unions
http://europa.eu.int/

International Court of Justice
http://www.icg cij.org/

World Trade Organizations
http://www.wto.org/

STATE LAW LOCATOR

State and Local Government on the Net
http://www.statelocalgov.net/

Municipal Codes
http://www.municode.com/

CHAPTER TWELVE

Sample Forms

This chapter contains a number of forms and letters which may be useful to your practice, or which may provide a starting point for developing forms of your own. Please remember that each state has its own laws and its own rules of professional conduct, and that what is permissible in one state may not be permissible in another. Review the requirements of your own state prior to using any form in this book.

Form 1

Sample Contingent Fee Agreement

ATTORNEY RETAINER AGREEMENT

On this the _____ day of _____, 200__, the undersigned retains and employs (name of law firm or attorney) as my/our attorney(s) to represent me/us with full authorization to do all things necessary in the investigation, litigation, and/or settlement of my/our claims against any and all parties arising from or related to my/our claims for the following:

_____

_____

For and in consideration of the above attorney(s) having agreed to represent me/us in this matter, I/we hereby agree to pay a contingent fee of _____ % of all monies recovered or obtained by settlement or judgment in this claim as a reasonable attorney's fee. In addition to the stated contingent attorney's fee, I/we also agree that my attorney(s) shall be reimbursed for all expenses and costs advanced on my/our behalf directly from the monies recovered by settlement or judgment.

I/We understand that no settlement will be made without my/our consent. I/we hereby agree not to settle, compromise, release, discontinue, or otherwise dispose of this claim without the consent and advice of my/our attorneys. I/we further agree not to meet with nor discuss this case with any representatives of the opposing party without my/our attorney(s) being present.

I/we hereby agree to cooperate fully with my/our attorney(s) in the preparation, settlement, and/or trial of this matter, to appear upon reasonable notice for depositions and court appearances, to keep my/our attorney(s) aware of my/our whereabouts at all times, to be honest and truthful with my/our attorney(s), and to comply with all reasonable requests made of me/us in the handling of this claim.

I understand that associate counsel may be employed at the discretion and expense of my attorney(s), and that any attorney so employed may be designated to appear on my attorney's behalf or undertake my/our representation in this matter.

I/WE HAVE READ AND THOROUGHLY UNDER-
STAND THIS CONTRACT AND HEREBY AGREE TO
ALL TERMS THEREIN.

Client Signature _____

Name: _____

Address: _____

City/State/Zip _____

Date: _____

Approved and agreed upon on this the ___ day of
_____, 200___.

_____

Attorney at Law

Form 2

Flat Fee Agreement

This flat fee contract is for use in criminal defense cases, but it can easily be adapted to fit other situations in which a flat fee is being charged by editing the appropriate provisions. Consult with your state bar association to determine whether your state would require certain terms to be included or removed.

CRIMINAL DEFENSE FEE CONTRACT

The undersigned client does hereby retain and employ (*attorney*) for representation on the following:

_____

_____

_____

    The undersigned client agrees to pay the sum of $ _____ as a fixed fee for representation in this matter. The undersigned understands that (*attorney*) will not begin work on this case until the fee has been paid in full, unless other payment arrangements have been agreed upon in writing and are set forth in this contract. The undersigned client agrees that this is a contract for services upon a fixed fee basis, and that the fee due from the undersigned client remains the same regardless of the length of time involved in the completion of services.

In the event that the parties have agreed upon payment arrangements in this matter, the terms of payment agreed upon are as follows:

_____

_____

_____

In the event that (*attorney*) has agreed to a payment plan in this matter, the undersigned client agrees that if client fails to pay the fees or costs as stated herein, then (*attorney*), shall be relieved of any further obligation to represent the client, and in that event (*attorney*) is authorized to withdraw from this case.

In addition to the above fee, the undersigned client agrees to pay all court costs, investigative fees, expert witness fees, deposition costs, all costs advanced, and any other out-of-pocket expenses directly incurred in investigating or litigating this case, and agrees that such expenses shall be paid in advance unless otherwise agreed. In the event that the undersigned client has not been required to pay certain expenses in advance, the client agrees to pay all such expenses within thirty (30) days of billing for the same.

In the event of nonpayment of the fee or expenses and the filing of suit to collect the same, the undersigned agrees to pay a reasonable attorney's fee and all costs associated with the suit for collection.

The fee quoted herein does not include any revocation hearings, or appeals or writs to a higher court, whether pre-trial or post-trial or whether initiated by the client or by the prosecution, or retrials following a mistrial, successful appeal, or where a motion for a new trial is granted. The client authorizes (*attorney*) to initiate any pre-trial appeal or writ if, in the attorney's opinion, the client's interests will best be served thereby. The undersigned client specifically authorizes (*attorney*) to take any action on his/her behalf, including the waiving of the right to a speedy trial or to a jury trial, if, in the attorney's opinion, the interests of the client would best be served thereby.

The undersigned client understands that associate counsel may be employed at the discretion and expense of the law firm, and that any attorney so employed may be designated to appear on the firm's behalf or undertake representation in this matter.

I,_____, have read and fully understand this contract, and I have discussed any questions I have with my attorney. I agree to the terms of this contract, and I have received a copy of this contract for my records.

Client Signature _____

Name:_____

Address: _____

City/State/Zip ————————————————

Date: ————————————————————

Approved and agreed upon on this the —— day of
—————, 200——.

————————————————————

Attorney at Law

Form 3

New Client Intake Sheet

Before ever meeting with a new client, it is advisable to have them fill out a basic information sheet. This will save time during your initial interview, and will ensure that you do not forget to obtain essential information (such as your client's phone number). It will be rare for someone to object to filling out such a form, since they are accustomed to this procedure at their physician's office. If client refuses or disputes the need to fill out such information, consider this the first red flag warning you that this may not be a person you want to represent.

Name: _____

Mailing Address: _____

City, State, Zip: _____

Date of Birth: _____

Social Security Number: _____

Home Phone: _____

Cell Phone: _____

Place of Employment: _____

Work Address: _____

Work Phone: _____

How did you hear about our firm?: _____

_____

Form 4

Divorce Information Questionnaire

The following questionnaire covers the typical information you will need to acquire when conducting an interview on a standard divorce case.

DOMESTIC RELATIONS INTERVIEW

CLIENT INFORMATION:

DATE: _____

_____

First Name Middle and/or Maiden Name Last Name

_____

Street Address

_____

City   State   Zip Code

Inside City Limits? _____

Usual Residence _____

State _____ County _____

How Long Have You Lived At This Address?_____

Home Phone _____

Date of Birth _____

Social Security Number _____

Employer _____

Employer's Address _____

Work Phone _____

Income $ _____ per_____

Job Title or Position _____

Last School Grade Completed _____

ADVERSE PARTY INFORMATION

_____

First Name Middle and/or Maiden Name Last Name

Street Address

_____

City   State   Zip Code

Inside City Limits? _____

Usual Residence _____

State _____ County _____

How Long Have You Lived At This Address?_____

How To Start A Successful Law Practice

Home Phone _____

Date of Birth _____

Social Security Number _____

Employer _____

Employer's Address _____

Work Phone _____

Income $ _____ per _____

Job Title or Position _____

Last School Grade Completed _____

MARRIAGE INFORMATION

Date of ceremony of present marriage _____

Place of ceremony of present marriage _____

_____

City   State   Zip Code

If you or your spouse have ever been married before, how many times?

You _____

Your Spouse _____

If previously married, how did last marriage end? (Divorce, Death, Annulment)

You _____

Your Spouse _____

Date the parties separated: _____

Last address at which you and your spouse lived together as husband and wife:

Address _____

City   State   Zip Code

How many children born of this marriage?

Name	Age	DOB	SS#

Names, ages, and birth dates of all children adopted by you and your spouse or which you or your spouse have custody of from a previous marriage:

Name	Age	DOB	SS#

_____

_____

_____

DIVORCE TERMS:

☐ Contested Divorce   ☐ Uncontested Divorce

Facts/Grounds causing you to want a divorce: (If TRO or PFA needed, state specific abuse)

_____

_____

_____

_____

_____

_____

Has client given up hope of "getting back together"?

_____

Wife to resume use of maiden name? ☐ yes ☐ no
If yes, change name to:

_____

Preference as to custody of children _____

Visitation desired (reasonable or special times)

_____

_____

_____

Who is to be allowed to claim the exemption for the children for income tax purposes?

_____

ALIMONY AND CHILD SUPPORT

Will either party voluntarily continue his/her insurance coverage on the children?
If so, which one?

_____

If not, should we seek this as part of what we ask the Court to order?

_____

Health insurance costs:

$ _____ per _____

Who is to pay for medical/dental expenses of the children not covered by insurance?

Husband Percentage: _____

Wife Percentage: _____

Child care costs: _____

$ _____ per _____

Does either party have pre-existing child suppor or alimony payment obligation?

If so, which party?

_____

How much? _____ per _____

Child support:

$ _____ per _____

Alimony:

$ _____ per _____

Payments due on:

_____

PROPERTY AND VALUE

Who will have ownership and/or be responsible for payment of debt (if applicable):

Real Estate	Value/Debt	Husband/Wife

Personal Property (automobiles, furniture, boats, etc.)

_____

_____

_____

_____

_____

_____

Special Items (jewelry, coin collections, silver, antiques, etc.)

_____

_____

_____

_____

_____

ASSETS:
BANK/ACCOUNTS/CDS/STOCKS/BONDS/IRA/
RETIREMENT/PENSION

_____

_____

_____

_____

LIABILITIES:
CREDIT CARDS/CREDIT UNION/BANK
LOANS/STUDENT LOANS

_____

_____

_____

_____

_____

_____

FOR ATTORNEY USE ONLY

Deadlines:
File Answer

_____

File Complaint:

_____

Fee agreed upon:

_____

☐ money received $ _____ ☐ retainer agreement
signed

Length of interview:

_____

Form 5

General Release of Records

This form is a general release of records, which includes a release for medical records. Under the new HIPPA guidelines, this form is no longer sufficient for obtaining records concerning a person's medical history. However, the form is still useful for obtaining documents from other sources, unless your state has imposed an additional local requirement on access to records.

RELEASE OF RECORDS

This form, or any photostatic copy hereof, authorizes all physicians, hospitals, medical attendants, employers, insurance companies, banks, bank employees, accountants, or any other persons or institutions to furnish to my attorneys, (attorney name and address), their associates or representatives, with full and complete information relating to the following, to wit:

_____

_____

_____

This authorization includes the right to examine any and all records, photographs, x-rays, account statements, and any other item or document, and the right to receive full and complete copies of information pertaining thereto, including copies of all such records.

ALL PRIOR AUTHORIZATION IS HEREBY CANCELLED

Signature: _____

Name: _____

Address: _____

City/State/Zip _____

Social Security Number: _____

SWORN TO and SUBSCRIBED before me on this the
_____ day of _____, 200_____.

_____

NOTARY PUBLIC
State of _____ at Large

PLEASE FORWARD REQUESTED COPIES TO:

(Name)

Attorney at Law

(Firm address & phone number)

Form 6

HIPAA-Compliant Medical Records Release

AUTHORIZATION TO USE OR DISCLOSE
PROTECTED HEALTH INFORMATION

I hereby authorize _____ to use or disclose the following protected health information from the medical records of the patient listed below. I understand that information used or disclosed pursuant to this authorization could be subject to redisclosure by the recipient and, if so, may not be subject to federal or state law protecting its confidentiality.

Patient Name:

_____

Social Security No.:

_____

Date of Birth:

_____

Address:

_____

City/State/Zip

_____

Information to be disclosed to:

(attorney name, address, phone number, fax number)

Disclose the following information for treatment dates:

_____

to

_____

☐ Complete Records   ☐ Consult

☐ Physical Therapy   ☐ Abstract

☐ Outpatient Reports   ☐ Emergency Reports

☐ Face Sheet   ☐ X-Ray

☐ Other Specified

_____

☐ Discharge Summary   ☐ Laboratory

☐ History & Physical   ☐ Pathology

The above information is disclosed for the following purposes:

☐ Medical Care   ☐ Legal   ☐ Insurance

☐ Personal   ☐ Other _____

_____ I understand I may revoke this authorization at any time by requesting such of the above referenced hospital/physician practice in writing, unless action has already been taken in reliance upon it, or during a contestability period under applicable law.

_____ I acknowledge, and hereby consent to such, that the release information may contain alcohol and drug abuse, psychiatric, HIV or genetic information.

_____ This authorization expires five (5) years from the date it was signed by the patient or the patient's authorized representative. Photocopies of this document will suffice for the original copy.

_____

Signature of Patient or Personal Representative

Date _____

_____

Printed Name of Patient

SWORN TO and SUBSCRIBED before me on this the _____ day of _____, 200 ____.

Pursuant to HIPAA Private Rule §164.508

Form 7

Limited Power of Attorney

In some circumstances, you will be required to present not only a release, but a power of attorney in order to gain access to certain client records. This form will provide access to most information you may need, or can easily be modified to suit your client's particular situation.

LIMITED POWER OF ATTORNEY

(*Name, date of birth, city and state of residence*) the Principal, hereby creates this Limited Power of Attorney for the purpose of enabling the Agent named below to act as the Principal's agent and attorney-in-fact for the limited purpose set forth in section 3 below.

1. **Designation of Agent**. The Principal hereby designates and appoints (*attorney*) of (*city, state*) to be the Principal's agent and attorney-in-fact to act in the Principal's name and stead for the limited purpose set forth in section 3 below.

2. **Effective Date**. This Limited Power of Attorney and powers conferred herein shall be effective as of the date of the execution of this Limited Power of Attorney by the Principal, which date is set forth below.

3. **Purpose of Power of Attorney**. The sole purpose of this Power of Attorney is to enable the Agent to act as the Principal's agent and attorney-in-fact for the limited function of (*purpose of limited power of attorney*).

4. **Power of Agent**. The Agent serving under this Limited Power of Attorney shall have all of the powers, rights, discretions, elections and authority confirmed by statute, the common law, or rule of court or governmental agency that are reasonably necessary to enable the Agent to carry out the purpose of this Limited Power of Attorney. In addition, the Agent shall have the following specific powers:

   A. The power to collect and receive all records, reports, funds, debts, monies, accounts, objects, interests, or demands due to the Principal in connection with the function described in section 3 above.

   B. The power to endorse the Principal's name for deposit into an account of the Principal in a financial institution with respect to any funds, checks, drafts or other sums payable to the Principal in connection with the function described in section 3 above.

   C. The power to sign, execute, seal, acknowledge and deliver any written document necessary or expedient to carry out the function described in section 3 above.

D.   The power to disburse, or to consent to the disbursement of, from the proceeds due to the Principal in connection with the function described in section 3 above, all expenses, charges or assessments customarily or properly payable by the Principal.

5. **Ratification**. The Principal hereby ratifies, acknowledges and declares valid all acts performed by the Agent in connection with the function described in section 3 above prior to the effective date of this Limited Power of Attorney.

IN WITNESS WHEREOF, the Principal has executed this Limited Power of Attorney on the day of ___, 20 __.

_____

(Name)

STATE OF _____COUNTY _____

Sworn to and subscribed before me on this the ___ day of _____,20_____, by

_____

_____

Notary Public

State of _____ at Large

Form 8

Fax Cover Sheet

DATE: _____

TO: _____

FAX #: _____

NUMBER OF PAGES (INCLUDING COVER PAGE)
_____.

FROM: _____ (Firm Name) _____

RE:

_____

_____

_____

_____

COMMENTS:

_____

_____

_____

_____

_____

_____

IF YOU HAVE ANY PROBLEMS RECEIVING THIS FACSIMILE, PLEASE NOTIFY_____ AT (123) 456–7890.

UNLESS OTHERWISE INDICATED OR OBVIOUS FROM THE NATURE OF THE TRANSMITTAL, THE INFORMATION CONTAINED IN THIS FACSIMILE MESSAGE IS ATTORNEY PRIVILEGED AND CONFIDENTIAL INFORMATION, INTENDED FOR THE USE OF THE INDIVIDUAL OR ENTITY NAMED ABOVE. IF THE READER OF THIS MESSAGE IS NOT THE INTENDED RECIPIENT, OR THE EMPLOYEE OR AGENT RESPONSIBLE TO DELIVER IT TO THE INTENDED RECIPIENT, YOU ARE HEREBY NOTIFIED THAT ANY DISSEMINATION, DISTRIBU-TION OR COPYING OF THIS COMMUNICATION IS STRICTLY PROHIBITED. IF YOU HAVE RECEIVED THIS TRANSMITTAL IN ERROR, PLEASE IMMEDI-ATELY NOTIFY US BY TELEPHONING (123) 456-7890 AND RETURN THE ORIGINAL TRANSMITTAL AT THE ABOVE ADDRESS VIA THE U.S. POSTAL SERVICE. WE WILL REIMBURSE YOU FOR ALL EXPENSES INCURRED. THANK YOU.

Form 9

Email Signature

In email communications, it has become standard for the attorney's name, firm name, address, and telephone number to be inserted at the end of the message automatically. Many now automatically insert legal disclaimers and/or notices regarding the contents of the message. The following sample disclaimers may be useful or relevant to your practice.

Example A:

Notice: This e-mail is covered under the Electronic Communications Privacy Act, 18 USC 2510–2521, and is legally privileged. The information contained in this e-mail is intended only for use of the individual or entity named above. If the reader of this message is not the intended recipient, or the employee or agent responsible to deliver it to the intended recipient, you are hereby notified that any dissemination, distribution or copying of this communication is strictly prohibited. If you have received this communication in error, please immediately notify us by telephone at the above number and destroy the original message.

Example B:

CONFIDENTIALITY NOTE: This e-mail and any attachments are confidential and may be protected by legal privilege. If you are not the intended recipient, be aware that any disclosure, copying, distribution or use of this e-mail or any attachment is prohibited. If you have received this e-mail in error, please notify us immediately by returning it to the sender and delete this copy from your system. Thank you for your cooperation.

Example C:

IRS CIRCULAR 230 DISCLOSURE: Any Federal tax advice contained herein is not written to be used for, and the recipient and any subsequent reader cannot use such advice for, the purpose of avoiding any penalties asserted under the Internal Revenue Code. If the foregoing contains Federal tax advice and is distributed to a person other than the addressee, each additional and subsequent reader hereof is notified that such advice should be considered to have been written to support the promotion or marketing of the transaction or matter addressed herein. In that event, each such reader should seek advice from an independent tax advisor with respect to the transaction or matter addressed herein based on the reader's particular circumstances.

Example D:

This e-mail may be privileged and/or confidential, and the sender does not waive any related rights and obligations. Any distribution, use or copying of this e-mail or the information it contains by other than an intended recipient is unauthorized. If you received this e-mail in error, please advise me (by return e-mail or otherwise) immediately.

Form 10

Settlement Disbursement Sheet

In a contingent fee case, it is important to disclose to the client exactly what money was received, what was spent, what is due to the attorney, and what is due to the client.

The example below contains a 33% attorney's fee calculation Note that 33% is not actually the same as a 1/3 attorney's fee. If you want your fee to actually be 1/3 of the recovery, either list it as 1/3 or as 33.33%.

Also note that some attorneys include a provision for a higher percentage (such as 40%) in their contract in the event the case actually proceeds to trial.

The following is a simple form for explaining a settlement disbursement, which should be customized for each client's situation.

ITEMIZATION OF SETTLEMENT DISBURSEMENT

(CLIENT)

Settlement received from Shelley Insurance	$18,000.00
Attorney's Fee 33%:	$ 5,940.00
Costs Advanced (Photocopies, facsimile, etc.)	$ 90.89
Medical Expenses Paid from Settlement: Igor Radiology	$ 40.75

Dr. Frankenstein $1,998.25

(*Attorney*) will draft checks directly to each of the above.

Balance to client: $ 9,930.11

I have read and understand the disbursement of the settlement proceeds in this case, and agree to settle the case upon these terms. I understand that I shall be responsible for making payment to those providers of medical services not listed above, if any.

_____

(Client)

Form 11

Collections Letter

Date _____

Addressee _____

Re: (company)

Dear :

I have been retained by (*client*) regarding your unpaid debt. All further contact regarding this matter should be directed to my office.

As you know, you obtained merchandise on credit from (*client*), but you have failed to pay your account. Your balance as of (*date*), including late charges, is *$XXXX.XX*. Late charges continue to accrue on this account at a rate of *$XX* per month, pursuant to the contract.

I have been instructed to take immediate action to collect the entire amount owed on this account. This letter is merely a courtesy on my part to give you an opportunity to pay without the additional expense and embarrassment of litigation. Please understand that this is not the first of a series of collection letters. If you do not respond to this letter, the next time you hear from me will be in a lawsuit against you. Please send a cashier's check or money order in the amount of *$XXXXX* made payable to me, as attorney for (*client*). If you do not make payment in full within thirty days of the receipt of this letter, I will use whatever legal procedures are necessary to collect this debt. I look forward to hearing from you soon.

Sincerely,

(*Attorney*)

NOTICE: This is an attempt to collect a debt. Any information obtained from you will be used in collecting this debt. Unless you dispute this debt or any portion thereof within thirty days after receipt of this notice, this debt will be assumed valid. If you notify me in writing within the thirty-day period that this debt or any portion thereof is disputed, I will obtain verification of the debt or a copy of the judgment against you and a copy of the verification of judgment will be mailed to you by me. Upon your written request within the thirty-day period, I will provide you with the name and address of the original creditor, if different from the current creditor.

About The Author

William L. Pfeifer, Jr., is an attorney who started his own law practice shortly after graduating from law school. He has practiced both with a partner and in a solo law office, and has firsthand experience in dealing with the challenges of starting a law firm. He is a frequent speaker at legal seminars and political events, has published numerous articles, and maintains a busy and successful law practice.